MORE THAN JUST

A

Feeling

Based on True Events

PREFACE

"You should write a book mate" That's what all my friends, acquaintances and people that pass through my life for a few months tell me.

So here it is, the book that I have been asked to write. I don't profess to be a professional author. However I do have a story to tell, and if you would like to hear it, read on. Open your heart and mind, and I promise you, you will gain something. Even if just one line of this book touches you, it will be worth the read.

I am a Welsh Man from humble beginnings born in the valleys of the South Wales. I am 1 of 8 children, the second from last. My parents have 4 girls and 4 boys. My sisters all came first, they were all born in the 70s and 80s. I remember the stories of how they would sneak out at night through their bedroom windows to punk rock parties at the age of 14 -15. No wonder my Dad had his first heart attack at the age of 40. My Mam said that when he was having his heart attack, my brothers and I were jumping on him because we thought he was play wrestling can you imagine. My poor Dad rolling around dying on the floor, and 2 of his 8 children jumping on him and

MORE THAN JUST A FEELING

dropping the big elbow on him. Goodness me, well he survived this one, his first of many Heart Attacks. You will learn of the others in the multitude of experiences that I will share with you throughout this book.

The sole purpose and intent of this book "More Than A Feeling" is to assist and help others like me. Like you, like anyone who has had ever had experiences that they can't really explain. These questions can lead to "Am I normal" "Why is life so hard" How does this happen" " What is this all about" "What's the purpose of me being here" "Does this happen to just me or anyone else too". "Where does this feeling come from".

This Book is going to open your eyes and bring you light when you're in a dark place. This book will instil hope back into the deepest part of your heart. This book will do exactly what it is meant to do, for you.... The reader.... THIS BOOK IS FOR YOU.

It may make you laugh, make you cry, make you wonder and make you realise that life is what it is, our personal legend, and if we accept and surrender to it, we can be made free.

I'm not an English expert, and I was kicked out of school at 14 years old. No qualifications. Please forgive the lack of literacy in this book. It's not intended to invigorate your natural mind with eloquence, but rather speak to your spiritual mind and heart.

BY N.D.H

Its intent is to help. Help you have HOPE. If you, like me, have had "the feeling" and have always followed it. Please never give up believing in its guidance, even when we don't understand why.

Introduction

To every man there openeth an highway and a low, the high man climbs the highway and Lowman gropes the low, and in between, on the misty flats the rest drift to and fro, but to every man there openeth a highway and a low, and every man decideth, the way his soul shall go.

Like I said, I was born in South Wales, I remember living in a small cul-de-sac called Snowden Court in a small town called Cwmbran. 8 Kids living in a small council house, bunk beds in every room, My Dad was a Barber! The best Barber in the whole town! He employed 2 Italian brothers I only remember 1 of their names, Vincenzo. My Dad used to say they would argue and threaten each other with the scissors, he had to stand in between them to stop them fighting. I remember going there and my Dad shaving mine and my brothers' heads, this was the 80s and one time I ran down the street after a fresh number 2 all over and I passed a group of skin heads, they shouted Oi SKIN HEAD ! So I ran a little faster.

There was a small woodland next to the cul-de-sac where we lived and we called it the Bluebell Woods, because of all the blue bells that grew there. At the back of the woods there was a river. I remember standing on the edge of the river one time after a few days of rain. The river was brown and running rough, at the age of 4-5yrs old this looked very scary. Then it came. The feeling, one of the very first times I felt It, or at least that I can remember feeling it. It felt like it said to me, "Don't go there, go back, and go home" But it had no words and no voice. But it felt warm and protective, like being surrounded in cotton wool. That was when I didn't really know what it was or why it came to me or could even understand what the Feeling was.

If you look back at your younger years, as a small child maybe you will recognise a similar thing. Maybe not as I have explained it, "like being surrounded by cotton wool" or a "voice with no words". But you will be able to remember something, something will come to your mind where you have maybe felt something like this, or similar.

My Dad sold the barber shop to Vincenzo! The mad Italian barber, and we moved to a small country town called Abergaveny. A beautiful little town, a big old Victorian Semidetached house, it had 4 floors and a basement.

This house was haunted. My brother said that one day he saw an old woman from the front window walking to the front door, and when he went to open it, there was no one there. My other brother said he saw an old woman looking out of the window on the third floor. My other older brother, told me that he came home drunk one night and a green orb came at him, and looked at him and went through the wall. This was the time of ghostbusters though. The same brother told me that he remembered watching TV and the dog started barking furiously at the wall. Well we moved from there to THE TOWN! THE TOWN of MERTHYR TYDFIL.

Did I mention that my Family is a religious Family?. Yes, we were. I am no longer involved in religion, and I will explain why in the following chapters. The street where we lived sat up on a hill of slag, from the old coal mines. It was a nice sort of street that was nestled between two of the roughest housing estates in the town. Swansea road and Twyncarmel. Boy oh boy I remember watching the fights out of my bedroom window as the drunks walked from estate to estate.

We have cold winters in Wales, and when it snows it snows. I remember one winter going for a walk on the slag heap with my brothers. I must have been around 6 years old. It was so cold, windy and foggy, and then again it came. The Feeling. Again it felt warm around my head neck and shoulders, and it said without a voice, "turn around and go home". I shouted to my brothers and they all said, "ok let's go". As the sight of our house came to view, the skies darkened as a blizzard storm came over us blocking our view of destination. We trudged on, shouting support to each other, "come on boys" "this way let's keep going" We were 5-6 years old remember, but we felt like were soldiers. We finally made it home and my Mother opened the back door and put as Infront of the potbellied wood fired stove she loved in the kitchen. We all warmed up, and I had a moment of peace, pondering on the Feeling or the Voice I had felt. I looked at my Mother and she looked at me, we smiled as if we both knew what I was thinking about and then it went. The moment went and we all got back into the busy family environment.

So there we have it, 2 of the very first experiences I had with the Feeling at a very young age. Little did I know of how the feeling I had felt would come to me again and again throughout my life, to guide, help, and heal me through life's great and joyous times, and throughout life's most difficult heart wrenching darkest times. But one thing I knew for sure was this. I had a feeling that came out of nowhere, and it spoke to me without words. I somehow understood the unspoken words, and when I did, I was guided, and kept safe.

CHAPTER 1

The Years from my childhood into my young adult life seemed to vanish. School was long and boring, and the daily routine of life was mundane, so I decided to play up a little. The day I met Daniels, my mate, we called him Elvis because he would sing Elvis songs. It was in the first year of high school he was in my new class, he had tropical fish and I had tropical fish, I had an angel fish that I did want any more so I asked him if he wanted it, he said yes, so I put this angel fish in a plastic bag with water and took it to his house, so you could say that it was an angel that brought us together.

We played up something terrible in school dancing to Shaggies Caroline on the tables, girls laughing and giving us the eyes, giggling incessantly at silly things, getting sent to the head teachers office almost every day.

School was still boring, and it wasn't long before I lost total interest. I never did any work, I never even brought my bag to school, I started smoking cigarettes, cigarettes turned into smoking dope, and then dope turned into LSD tabs. We had a group of friends we started to hang out with, they were a bit posh, as they lived over the posh area, and it was a 15 min walk to their area along the back of our street, on a stony road that lead to a small tip that had a pathway from constant foot traffic.

My brother in law at the time smoked dope and I used to get it from him, we would sit in a small cabin at the bottom of our mates house we called it Bobs cabin we all got smashed in there all night and my brother and I would walk home through the dark tip area and along the stony road past the rough housing estate paranoid and walking fast, through the rain and wind to get home. We would get home stoned and walk into the living room and stand there giggling, my Dad would say disappointedly "Ah there they are! Bill and Ben the flowerpot men" We would laugh and hurry into the kitchen to make a cheese and ham toasties, the best munchie satisfier ever.

The following course of events changed my life forever. One night my brother and I decided to take an acid tab, we didn't feel it come up and decided to take another, we started laughing and feeling the butterflies come up in our bellies, we decided to go around my mate's house, and have a drink with the boys. As we were laughing and having a bit of fun, someone happened to mention that it was FRIDAY the 13th! DA DA DAAAA…. Like a ton of bricks, the trip dropped on me I immediately fell into a state of dread and immediately knew something bad was going to happen at 12 midnight. I kept telling everyone and they just laughed, thinking I was just tripping and freaking out, but I knew deep in my gut that on 12 midnight, something was going to happen. The boys decided to go out to the town to drink. My brother and I said we will stay, because we were both tripping out and needed to be in doors. One of my friends stayed with us as he thought he should look after us because my brother and I were tripping out pretty bad, my brother was seeing bubbles rise up from the floor and I was still sure that something was going to happen. I had this feeling of dread intensify as the night went on. My friend decided to go out to get more beers so it was just my brother and I left in the house, we both tried to console each other saying that it will be ok, and we will come down soon so we just tried to sit there and wait it out. My friend came back with beers, he was pretty drunk by this time, and I kept telling him that something was going to happen at 12 ! I just knew it! There was an old coocoo clock on the wall with a pendulum swinging side to side, the feeling of dread intensified to an uncontrollable state ! The clock read 11.55pm and I was freaking out to the point that I went to the kitchen a grabbed a big knife and sat on the sofa. I grabbed a cushion, so I was armed with a shield and a sword ! 11:59pm came, I looked at my brother and he looked at me, and I looked at my drunken friend and he was a little nervous at my disposure, 12 midnight struck and the coocoo clock chimed, then, the doorbell rang DING

DONG!

I looked at my drunken friend who I had been telling something would happen all night and his eyes grew wide and his mouth dropped open. I stood up armed and ready to face what was haunting me all evening, my friend opened the door as I stood behind him as adrenaline and the courage to face the axe man filled my whole body. As the door opened, it was all the boys coming back from town drunk and merry !! POP! The tension burst like a balloon and the fear and dread left me. I put the knife down and we smoked a couple of joints to bring us all down. My friend, my brother and I were still amazed at how I knew something was going to happen at 12 midnight and that was the exact time the boys came back from town.

This little freaky experience made me realise that there are other forces at work, forces that I had no clue about. I believed that it was an evil force, a force that wanted to let bring fear and dread show itself in the natural world to me. This force crossed the line from a paranoid acid trip, into a real-life scenario.

Although this experience had a profound effect upon me, I had no idea what effect it had had upon my older brother, his life was to be changed forever, his life would turn from being popular with all the girls and a steadfast strong gentleman, to a life of uncertainty.

It goes like this. A few months passed, I laid off the acid for a while and just smoked dope. School was becoming so boring for me that I would hardly go to any lessons. I was 14 and pre-GCSE mock tests were being held. I had no interest whatsoever in gaining any sort of mark, I remember just ticking any box so I could just get out of there. One-time Daniels was sitting next to me and we were making each other laugh, the teacher at the front saw us and kicked us both out ! Daniels was a little mad at me because he wanted to go to uni, and I didn't have any ambition for study at all. One morning I walked into school and the head teacher called me into his office and asked said to me "you don't want to be here do you" I said "no sir" he said "then go home and don't come back" I was 14years old.

Wow... I was released from the torment of the teachers, the constant negativity of their prideful remarks. One teacher always used to tell me that I will be sweeping the streets ! Well in some case it turned out that I did, but for a lot more money than the teachers were earning that's for sure.

I went home and told my mother, I thought she would hit the roof, but her shoulders fell with relief and she said "oh well never mind"

At around this time my Dad had another heart attack and was rushed in for another triple bypass. He came out of hospital skint. My mother worked 5 nights a week as a Geriatric nurse to support the

8 children and pay the mortgage. As my Dad recovered, he decided to open another barber shop, a trade that he thought he had left behind.

My Mam asked me to help him, so I did. Little did I know that this time with my Dad, would be one of the best learning experiences ever, his positivity was never ending ! The first day we opened we had 5 customers, we charged $4 a haircut. This is where I learnt how to cut hair, I would go out to get the morning papers and tissues, sneak into the public toilets to roll a joint and smoke it on the way back to the shop. Sometimes I would get back stoned and my Dad would ask me to do a haircut, Number 1 all over ! They were my haircuts, I would laugh and hope my Dad didn't know I was stoned. I would practice on my school friends, and my brothers and began to get pretty good. My Dad paid me $5 per day, so when I learnt I could earn $150 a week working as a labourer I did. I left the shop and went to work construction. I felt a little sad leaving my Dad on his own, but it was ok because my younger brother got expelled from school also, and he ended up working with my Dad, he became the best barber you would ever know, all the gangsters in the town would come to him, knew absolutely everyone.

Anyway my construction job took me away to work on a big concrete pile foundation job, it was amazing I loved it! I would get up at 5am work all day on jack hammers and shovels, eat good food and sleep at 8pm. This continued, money came in and I was happy, until one day I received a call from my mother saying my older brother is in the mental hospital and isn't very well and could I come home? I was worried, as I knew he still wasn't right after our Friday the 13th acid trip.

I asked my boss, and he said I could go. I went home and went straight up to St Tydfil's, that was the name of the hospital. I walked in and saw both of my parents sitting next to my brother trying to console him, I looked at my brother and he looked at me, he was sitting there skinny and grey, his legs bouncing and mouth open, his hands were on his legs facing up and I could see that he had tried to cut his wrists. He stammered "Alright Mate" at which I was overcome with emotion and fled out of the door so I could hide my tears.

After gathering myself back together, I went back in and walked up to my brother put my arms around him and held him, I said "Aright Mate, Alright"

6 months he was in there for, 6 long months. He was diagnosed as schizophrenic and his life would never be same. He came out and tried to stab himself with a world war 2 Banet, it hit his hip bone. A few weeks later he tried to hang himself from the stairs, but the rope broke, his neck was bruised all around. We all slept with the doors open at night so we could hear if he was up. We hid all the knifes and ropes and anything dangerous he could harm himself with, the boy was only 16 -17 years old. My parents didn't

sleep for months. Looking back at this time, I realise that my parents held onto my brother's life with all the might and courage of facing 10 thousand warriors. AND THEY WON. The medicine finally built up in his system and calmed him down, the medicine started to work and life for him and my family became a little more peaceful. Until…

Well we have a family of 8 you know, so when something is going on with one , something always goes on with another, as the eyes were on my big brother, my little brother had some problems. He was smoking dope, taking drugs and playing up around the estate, his best friend was the main drug dealer of one of the estates, my little brother was only around 13 -14 years old. One day I went out the back of the house for a cigarette, it was late afternoon and half way through my smoke, my little brother came around from the side of the house, and said "I've done something" I said "what ?" he said "promise not to tell Mam and Dad" ,, I said "ok.. what's up little bro" he handed me a bottle of empty pills and said I just ate all of these, it was a bottle of 400mls tabs of ibuprophen! I immediately threw the bottle on the floor and it smashed, I grabbed him by the scruff, and dragged him in doors and shouted to my Mam to call an ambulance, she said "why what's wrong" I told her what happened. An ambulance came, and we rushed him in, he had his stomach pumped and had to drink this black charcoal liquid, he went out for the count and the doctor said" let's hope he comes around and that he hasn't doesn't any damage inside"

I stayed with him as long as I could. One evening I went there, and he was on his own, he was awake, and we went for a walk down the hospital corridors. We talked and we talked, he asked me what he should do ? And then it came. The Feeling, this time it was very strong, it flooded my body and my voice changed as I spoke to him, my whole body tingled and all the hairs on my head stood on end. I'm not too sure what I said to him, but his face lit up, and I could see that his body was being filled with light and hope. To this day he relates to this experience and tells me that when I was talking to him, my face was shining, and my eyes were on fire. But all I knew was that I was feeling the feeling that I had felt before. Hope was restored to my younger brother, and his life changed and flourished, for the moment peace was restored to the Family.

So, what is this feeling and where does it come from? How does it come? How does it know when to come? People have their own beliefs about spirituality and God and the Universe and Energies etc, and I have my own, my very own and they will stay my own as to not open my sacred belief to the ridicule of the world. What I can say, is that it is not of this world or dimension, but it is aware of every single thing in this world, to the perfect detail of a single leaf falling from a tree, in every part of this world.

It knows the detailed timing of events that were set before the world was even populated. It is aware of every heart, every intention and every thought. It is sacred, it is all powerful and it can do things that would be incomprehensible to our limited imaginations. Is it the same force that assisted Moses in parting the red sea ? Is it the same energy Moses saw in the burning bush ? Is it the same love that caused the blind to see and the lame to walk? If so, where does it come from where does it reside and how does it know the future ? The past ? And the present ? I know what some of you are thinking. Your thinking its God or Jesus or The Holy Spirit. My thoughts shall remain my own and I will let you make your own mind up, but as you will see in the coming chapters and events that follow, this energy continues to manifest itself throughout my life.

CHAPTER 2

Remember I told you that I was raised in a religious family. Well at the age of 18 every young boy is expected to go on a mission for 2 years. This chapter will be a description of the events that led me to serve a mission and the experiences that I had during the 2 years I spent in Scotland as a missionary.

I was about 18 – 19 years old. I still worked construction and went out on weekends taking speed and dancing in the nightclubs. Speed is a terrible drug, the comedowns are horrific and depressing. One weekend I remember dancing for 2 days, and I woke up in a house that smelt of cats, on a dirty mattress on the floor. I got up and walked out of there. I walked the streets early morning just before dawn, and I remember feeling that this cannot go on and I need to change this pattern of behaviour. I felt like tar on the inside, I felt dark and depressed, the sun rose, and I walked home. I showered and dressed in comfortable clothing and sat in the living room with my Mother and Father, the words going through my mind that I need to change I need to

MORE THAN JUST A FEELING

change.

Two men knocked the door, and my Father answered, "Come in" he said, and in walked 2 missionary's form the church. They came in and sat down, at this time I would have usually got up and walked out of the room, but for some reason I stayed.

The 2 missionaries talked with my parents and I just looked busy and didn't want to make eye contact. Then I realised that one of them kept looking at me, I felt a little paranoid and got a little uncomfortable. I was about to say to him "What the bloody hell you looking at me for mate" but before I did, he looked at me and said "if you want to change, read this book". I said to myself, "How did he know that I wanted to change ?" and "Who told him to say those words ?" "Where did that come from ?" I was a little concerned until I realised that he must have been feeling the feeling, the feeling without a voice but it tells you what to say or do.

I acknowledged him with a nod of my head and said thank you. He gave me the book and held onto it.

The 2 missionaries went on their way and I took the book to bed.

How did he know I wanted to change? Do I really want to change? What would it mean if I did change? What would my life be like? I was up all night looking at the book he gave me, at the bottom of my bed, wondering if I really wanted to read it. He said that if I wanted to change, which I did , that this book would change me. If I read it, would I really change? I started to believe, that if I read it, I would change. How else would he know what I had been thinking all day?

1am came and I was wide awake, still pondering upon the change I wanted and worried what this book would do if I read it.

I finally gave in, I kicked the sheets off me and flipped around, so my head was at the bottom of the bed, I turned on a lamp and said, "Right then, let's see what going to happen".

The sheets were over my head the room was dark, other than the small lamp over the book. It was about 2am in the morning by now, and everyone was sleeping. So I built up the courage and opened the book fully expecting that something was going to happen. I started reading a few sentences, and then something started to happen, something so soft and gentle, the feeling came. It flooded over my body from my head down my neck and shoulders and over my face. It felt warm and comforting. The hairs on the back of my head stood up, and I could feel my breath changing. I now recognise that this was the same feeling that came to me on occasions before. No sooner than the feeling had filled my body, I started to read again, but something very very strange was happening. As I was reading to myself in my mind, the voice in my head began to change. It was as if the author of the words I was reading was speaking to me in my head ! I was astounded, and my eyes open wider and wider, I kept reading, and the voice began to be more intense. I could hear the authors sincerity, I could hear the authors concern and his authenticity of his desire to express what he was trying to tell the reader. The book was shining into my face and it felt like I was looking into a magical world, a world of truth and light. The more I read the more I understood the authors concern for the welfare of mankind. His sincerity struck me deep down, deep within my soul. I read, and I read, and then realised that the sun began to rise, and morning was here. I had read for hours but it only seemed like a moment.

I closed the book and got up and ran downstairs. I shouted to my Mam and Dad, and said " hey ! do you realise the power of this book ?" and began to tell my parents what had happened. My Dad almost chocked on his breakfast and said we know son we know, and they both beamed with delight that I had now began to know. The smiles and love that filled the breakfast room that morning whilst I was trying to explain to them how I felt, and what had happened that night was like I had won a million dollars and we were all celebrating.

Time went on and I felt clean inside. I felt that the darkness and dirty tar like feeling inside me had been taken away. I felt happy, and that happiness showed as I spoke to people in the streets ,as I spoke to friends and family, I was happy and confident in everything I did.

CHAPTER 3

It came time for me to decide if I wanted to go on a mission myself, and to be a missionary. As I thought on the decision I reflected on the missionary that told me that if I wanted to change, I should read this book, and if I could help someone the way he helped me then it would be worth it. So, I decided that I would go.

It took weeks and weeks before I was told where I would be going. Then when I was told where I was to go, there was only a few shorts weeks before it was time for me to go. I went to Scotland!

Saying goodbye to my family, my younger brother and my older brothers and sisters was a little unnerving, who was going to look out for them? Who was going to talk to them when they were feeling down? But I felt a reassurance that it was going to be fine. My parents took me and dropped me off at the training centre. It was time to say goodbye to them, I remember the tears of my Mother, and I said to her "Mam, please don't cry I'm going to be ok". You know that when you go on a mission, you're not allowed to speak to your family for 2 years, only through letters. So I think that this is why my

Mother was crying, she knew we wouldn't see each other for 2 years, and we had been there for each other through my older brothers' mental illness until he became stable. Through many other bonding experiences, you know that with my very first paycheck working construction, I took my mother out shopping and bought her a dress, I felt so proud to be able to do that, she still has the dress to this this day.

Anyway, we said goodbye and I was on my own, I was met by the President of the mission and his wife. I remember him being tall and bald, and a very serious man. He owned a major construction company in America and wore a big gold ring with a huge diamond. His hands were massive, he grabbed my and shook it, and laid down the law. Little did he know that was not like the other missionaries, all the spoilt little rich American boys playing popular. I was a Welsh boy who took lots of drugs and partied hard. I was street smart, and knew a fake American when I saw one. However saying that I knew a genuine American when I saw one to, and I must say I met a lot. So was put to work, I had to go and knock on strangers' doors from 9am until 9pm every single day. Having the door slammed in your face all day everyday was enough to beat the light out of anyone. But we continued trying to laugh and make some fun out it. I moved around a bit , and partnered up with different missionaries traveling

BY N.D.H

through Scotland. But this one time, I met a family that had 3 girls! Wow they were all lovely and good looking and our age, being a Welsh man I have obviously been blessed with charm. I open my mouth and it just comes out! I don't know where it comes from, but I had lines for sure. I had become familiar with the girls and had great fun with them. You're not allowed to kiss any girls on this mission, and I can say that I did not I was a very good lad, but I wanted to! I got a bit close to one of them and my missionary partner became jealous, and reported me to the mission President. I was banished to the furthest part of Scotland! The Shetland Islands! Oh my goodness, I had to live in the smallest room with a guy I didn't even like, I tried to make friends with him but man, some people you just can't make friends with. It was Christmas time, and my family had sent me a Christmas package. I stayed up until midnight Christmas eve and opened the box and celebrated Christmas on my own, a very sad situation when your used to a family of 8 at Christmas. Everyone running around talking cooking and having fun, and there I was on my own in the middle of the North bloody sea!

I would call the girl on the phone when the guy I was sharing with was asleep, and we said how we missed each other, and that I would come and see her when I could, and all that sort of stuff. The mission would get the telephone bills, and would see where I was phoning, so I just sent $10 to the mission president and told him I was using the phone and making calls, and there was the money for it ! Well he sent it back and said its ok just don't do it again, but I did, and I did. The guy told on me, and again I was banished to be junior under the snottiest, ass licking, tell-tale American missionary you could of ever imagined. He was to report my every move to the president. That's why I was sent there, because the president knew that this guy would take delight in telling on me. Man! I was sad, I was SOOO sad. I felt betrayed, I felt sick and I felt so disappointed in this whole mission thing. All I wanted to do was help someone like I was helped, and this is how I was being treated. It was enough for me to tell them all to stick it and go home. I was at my darkest moment, doubt filled my insides, disappointment pulled my shoulders and head down, I went quiet and wouldn't speak to anyone. Until one day, we were all called to a mission conference, this would be a meeting of around 250 guys, just like me in a big hall and the president would talk, and teach us things, and give us training. I sat there wondering what the hell I'm still doing here, feeling that I'm amongst people I don't even like, when suddenly the mission president started to talk, and everyone went quiet. I lifted my head with a doubtful heart, and began to try and listen to what he was saying. Then it came, yes it came to me again, the feeling. But this was like no other time it had come before, it was like time suddenly stood still, everything was in slow motion. I looked up at the ceiling. As I gazed up at the ceiling, I saw a light hovering above the congregation. It was as though I was the only one that could see it. Then, as I was looking at the light, a portion of the light left the main body of the light, and slowly travelled down towards me. I watched it, and sat still not moving a muscle except my head, as I watched this portion of light travel down towards me. The light moved slowly and calmly. I watched it as it entered into my chest. A part of the main body of light, came down and actually entered into my chest! I could not believe what I was seeing, but it was there, I saw it happen with my own eyes. Immediately after this had happened, I felt the darkness, doubt, fear and disappointment become displaced by this light that had entered into my chest. My eyes were wide, and my mouth was open, and my body was filled with light again!

Everything turned around, I began to like this telltale goody goody I was put with. He didn't like me, but I liked him anyway! I would get up in the morning and work hard. I worked, I worked, and I worked, with a happy smile and happy disposition. Slammed doors were a pleasure, people calling me names in the street was amazing, everything was going so well.

Then, late one evening we were knocking on doors and buzzing on buzzers. We were in a pretty rough area of Scotland, and we were tired. I buzzed a buzzer, and was about to walk away when a lady opened a window about 4 stories up, she shouted down and said, "What do you want ?" I said the spiel that we were trained to say. You know the hardest thing to sell is religion and we were basically salesmen for the church.

So, she shouted down and said, "what you want?" I shouted up and said, "Hey I have a book for you, it will change your life" she said "Ah I haven't got time tonight, come back another time" so I said "Are you sure Miss, this is going to change your life?" "Ahhhh" she said, "ok come on up."

We both went up to the 4th floor, she opened the door and said, "come in" After a few formalities' and building up a relationship of trust, through building on common beliefs, we sat down on the sofa and she sat opposite us on a small chair. It was like she was interviewing us. She asked us questions, we answered best we could, and then it happened. I pulled out this book and held it in my hand. I looked at her, and before I could say anything, the room became electrified. The room became thick with an energy I hadn't felt so intense before, it was almost tangible. The feeling came, so gracefully and gently it filled my whole body. I was feeling this energy so strongly and I knew that this lady was feeling it also, because her eyes widened, and her mouth was open. I spoke, and my voice was different, it had a smoothness to it, I could hear it myself. I told the lady about the book and how it could change her life as it did mine. As I was speaking she started to lean back into the chair, and the chair was leaning back on its back legs. She went so far back that the back of the chair fell against the wall. As the energy started to disperse, the lady came back from leaning up against the wall and the chair fell back onto all four legs again. The room was silent for a few wonderful moments, she broke the silence and said "Wow, that was powerful! Where did that come from ?"

We went our ways and keep InTouch to this very day.

The mission came to an end and I went home, I flew to Manchester and my mother screamed when she saw me come through the gate and then she ran and grabbed me! I was home.

CHAPTER 4

Now, let's stop here for a moment and examine the Feeling the Energy and the Light that had come, and keeps coming to me through my life. Let's see what and why and when and where, before I go onto to tell you about the further experiences of the feeling that continues to come to me. That has guided me, protected me, and comforted me throughout my life.

Some of the greatest teachers of spirituality say that our bodies our like Temples. Temples are places where the spirit of God, or Universal Energy can enter. Temples have been built throughout the ages all over the world. So many cultures of humanity understood or believed, that Temples are Holy Places, where communication to and from a Higher source of energy can be sought after.

If our bodies are like Temples, can this mean that a Higher Energy, the spirit of God or the Energy of the Universe can enter? This question is for you to answer.

Why would a Higher Universal Energy want to enter our bodies, or our lives to guide us, comfort us, direct us and protect us? Could it be that it has an interest in us? An interest in our lives and our wellbeing? Why would it? And how does it know how we are feeling, where we are, and what we are doing?

Again, many Spiritual leaders say that the Spirit of God is Love. The Highest Energy is Love, and that we are all part of the Universal Energy. If we are part of this Universal Energy, then are we not part of this Love also ?

I had a little experience once, where I closed my eyes in nature, and I saw that every living thing. Trees, grass, animals and ourselves, when stripped of the outer form, inside was all light. Not like a like from a light bulb, but a translucent light. All the translucent light of every living thing was connected. It was all joined together into the earth. We were all part of one main light or Energy. Energy is or has intelligence, or is intelligence Energy? This question I don't know. However every living thing has been given more intelligence than others. Every living thing fulfils the purpose of its creation. For example, a tree, a tree grows and leaves bud and blossom. The blossoms distribute pollen. Bees, butterflies drink the nectar from the pollen in each tree or flower and by going tree to tree, or flower to flower, pollinates the trees and flowers. This process allows the seeds within to become pollenated, and then the seeds from the flower or tree become fertile, then they scatter, and plant within the ground to grow a another. This is the cycle of its purpose, it does it and that's it, that's what it does. Does it have a choice? and say "no, not this year, I don't feel like it." No, it obeys its purpose of creation and does what its designed to do.

Now, as we go up the chain, to say animals. It could be said that they have choices, the bull can say "no thank you, I'm not going through that gate into that field, the grass is better here." The dog, dog owners know that every dog is different, and they say that they have "personalities". If this is the case, then the level of intelligence in animals could be a little more than the intelligence in trees and flowers? Maybe they have a little choice?

The Chimpanzee and Gorilla, this is very interesting, and I really don't know the answer here, but I do know that Chimpanzees could talk just like humans, but their vocal cords are set lower in their throats, this will not allow them to control their vocal cords to talk. Why is this? They communicate to us through sign language. They learn Sign language for goodness sake, how much intelligence does that take, that's a lot of intelligence for sure. Does the higher source of Universal Energy enter these and guide, direct, protect and comfort these animals? Possibly, who would know? It could be said that it does. When you live closely to one of these animals, you can feel its energy, its personality. Koko the female gorilla for example, her owner taught her sign language. The Gorilla communicated with humans. The Gorilla would express sadness, happiness and express love through this source of commination. If a Gorilla can express love, where does this love come from?

Maybe the Universal Energy, that is part of all living things, is pure and unconditional love. If that love is within all living things, then are we not love also?

Now we have the Human. The Human is a little bit different than all the rest. The level of intelligence within the Human, is far superior than any of the levels of intelligence in any other living thing on this planet. Humans have found a way to control other livings things, like trees and animals. We seem to have asserted authority over all other living things. Take the Bull for example, the bull does not want to go through the gate into the other field. So the Human caged the bull, put a ring through its nose, which is not very nice. The human can pull the bulls nose ring, that hurts the bull and the bulls walks forward as to not feel that pain. It is then guided by the human into the field that it didn't want to go. The Dog again for example, a dog is a little bundle of joy and happiness as a puppy, jumping around playing, eating, drinking, having no worries at all, laying sleeping when tired etc. However, the Human again has found a way to train the dog for its purpose, maybe to hunt, and to guard the human from dangers.

What I'm trying to get at is this. All livings things have an energy. All living things are part of the same energy. The Universal Energy, it is one. However, it could be said that all living things have been given different levels of Energy or intelligence in order to fulfil its purpose of creation.

If all living things have a purpose of creation, and have different levels of Intelligence, what purpose does the Human have? What is my purpose? What is your purpose?

Are we supposed to just try and control all the other levels of intelligence and manipulate them for our benefit? Or is there something deeper, more meaningful?

The Buddhists believe in re-incarnation. Other religions do not.

Can I offer a perspective on both?

What if the sole purpose of all energy is to progress to become like the highest source of intelligence, or Universal Energy.

What does this mean and how would it happen? If the energy, or intelligence within a tree comes out of the tree when the tree dies, where does it go ? Does it go to heaven and become a tree? It could do but how do we know? The Buddhists believe it could come back as an ant or a dog? And again, if the energy or intelligence of a dog comes out from the dog when the dog dies, does it go to heaven and become a dog, or does it come back as a gorilla?

Am I suggesting the reincarnation of Spirit or Energy until it reaches its perfect state? Is this what is described as reaching Enlightenment? Or becoming a Universal Energy ourselves? Having the power to create energy and assisting the energy we create along the path of progress until it becomes like us, and thus, we also grow in glory and love, whilst still belonging to the Universal Energy that created us. increasing its glory.

You can see where I'm going with this now can't you. What if, all energy or intelligence has the sole purpose of becoming the ultimate source of intelligence. This would mean that all energy or intelligence would continue to progress until it has received perfection, and become part of the ultimate Universal Energy, the energy that is indeed the universe. What if I put it to you, that the Universal Energy cannot progress past perfection, because perfect is perfect ! However the only way that it can progress, would be through its glory and power being added to and added to by all the energies it has created, becoming like itself and being added too, growing in perfectness and glory forever and ever. The work of the Universal Energy could be to bring all energy and intelligence to be like itself, perfect. This way, the Universal Energy grows and grows in glory and love and this being an eternal process, the universal energies glory is unfathomable to our limited minds. If we open our minds to this thought, and look into this way of progression to perfection, we would look at each other and all living things on this earth so differently. We would

MORE THAN JUST A FEELING

see that we are all on this journey, the journey towards perfection or enlightenment together. We would see that the energy or level of intelligence in animals and tress, that is a little less than ours, will one day become like ours. Would we not want to love them and help them fulfil their purpose? Would we not want our fellow humans to walk side by side, with us on this journey? Or if they are struggling lend a hand to pull them up? Or if they are ahead cheer them on? Would we not be filled with love and hope towards all living things?

This opens a perspective. A perspective on the way we see energy, the way we see others and other living things on this planet. The way we feel towards the energy and its intent towards us. The Universal Energy wants us to become like it, and wants to help us become like it. For me this shows that the Universal Energy is pure love and light, and looks at us mere mortals and sees the potential within each living thing on this planet.

How confident we can be, when a perfect energy sets out to perform a work, the work being to bring to pass the immortality, glorification and eternal life of all energy on this planet. I'm pretty much convinced that it will carry out its work in all perfectness. How else can a perfect energy work? Only perfectly right?

Is the Universal Energy come from a being or is it just an energy force that looks like light?

BY N.D.H

Can I share with you something that happened to me, that makes me believe the Universal Energy comes from a being?

I went to a grand opening and dedication of a Temple. I was about 19 years old, and my family travelled together, for 4 hours from Wales to Preston.

The opening and dedication attracted thousands of people. My family and I hustled into a church phew and we all sat together. There were talks given by the Church leaders and prayers offered, it was all kind of normal and a little boring to be honest, until the closing Hymn.

It was customary in these dedications, that a certain hymn would always be sung by the congregation. It's called "The Spirit of God, Like a Fire is Burning".

We were all asked to stand. I stood up with the hymn book in front of me, and started to sing. My Dad was right next to me, and we looked at each other and belted out our good Welsh Voices. There were thousands of people singing, and when you're in a congregation of people singing, the atmosphere is always amazing. The hairs on my neck stood on end, and I felt great. It was very similar to the feeling that would come to me. The singing was absolutely amazing! Then suddenly the church hall became electrified, all the hairs on my body were stood on end, and I stopped singing. The feeling came to me, it flooded my whole body like it always

MORE THAN JUST A FEELING

had before. It was so powerful that I could not sing any more, but still the singing was amazing. Tears flowed down my checks due to the overwhelming emotions flooding my body. I looked over to my Dad, and saw that he was overcome also. He wasn't singing either, but still the singing was so beautiful, it was like we were all professional singers in a magical choir. Thousands of voices all singing in harmony, so perfectly. I couldn't even speak, and tears were still flowing down my cheeks. I looked around at the congregation, and saw that no one was singing, but they all had their heads down being overcome with the same feeling that I was having. But still the singing went on, it was so beautiful, women's high pitch notes, men's deep gallant tones all in unison and harmony, and so loud!

I couldn't believe what I was hearing, and I couldn't believe that I was hearing this and everyone I looked at wasn't signing! Where was this magical chorus coming from? Just as I thought I would be totally overcome, the song finished on a beautiful, strong harmony and then it stopped. There was total silence in the congregation. We all stood for just a few more moments and then we all sat down. The feeling dispersed and my Dad looked over at me and said "Wow, son, I don't know where all that beautiful singing was coming from because I didn't sing a word" I said, "Me neither Dad".

As we all started to leave the building, everyone was muttering to each other telling each other the exact same thing as my Dad and me.

I believe, the heavens opened for a few moments, and the singing that we heard was the voices of other beings, that we could not see with our natural eyes.

If this is the case, then what does this mean? Are there other beings? Are there angels? What do they look like? If they can sing like we can sing, could they look like us?

The scripture, "God created man after his own image: may have some real context to it.

They also say, that "God is Love"

What does this mean? If we look like God, and God is Love then does this mean that the Universal Energy comes from God, a being? A being that can fill space and time? That knows all things?

I know what I think, and I know what I choose to believe.

If you agree or disagree, does not matter to anyone except yourself, as really our thoughts and beliefs are our very own, and we do indeed own them.

CHAPTER 5

Now, let's move on to the time where I have completed my mission, and have returned home. I returned home to the Welsh Valleys. A very strange feeling, because I was regimented. I had been following a regime for 2 years and now suddenly I was back home and expected to live normal life. On leaving the mission, my mission president said to me "Now go home and get married" So, that's what I thought I should do right?

I had no job, no routine to follow, it was a little unnerving. By this time my sister had taken over my Fathers Barbershop. He still worked there. My little brother also left school at the age of 14 and again my Dad took him into the Barber shop to teach him the trade So my little brother, my sister and my Dad worked together in the barber shop. I asked my sister if she could employee me there also? She agreed and spent valuable time and money on teaching me to cut men's hair to a standard of acceptance for the shop's reputation, which was very high.

The Barber shop that my Dad opened more than 6 years ago went from just him and me, cutting 3-5 haircuts a day, and maybe 1-2 skin heads by me, when I was mostly stoned, to a shop that had 4 family members cutting all day every day. We would see how many we all did at the end of every day. My sister would always win, I tried and tried to beat her numbers, and worked and worked, I even got my haircut time down to 7 mins, good quality to, but my sister would always win, she made it look so easy. The shops reputation was phenomenal, customers would travel 30 miles to get a haircut. Of course my little brother new absolutely everyone in the town, he had all the towns gangsters coming in, he never got in trouble with anyone because of his network.

We took on a young Turkish barber, he was very good too, the shop was doing fantastic, 5 people cutting all day every day. My older brother who wasn't well even started to work with us, sweeping the floors and taking the register, 5 family members and a little Turkish man working together. What a success the shop became. As you can see, from small and simple things, great things are brought to pass. With a hope in your heart and a positive mindset, growth does happen, in whatever avenue we decide to focus our minds on.

One day, we had a call from our Mother, that our Dad was suffering another heart attack. I rushed up to the house, to see him walking to the ambulance. I got into the back of the ambulance with him and the sirens blasted as the ambulance ducked and dived through the traffic. Then it came again, the feeling, it entered all my body, and said to me to lay my hands on his head, and ask for him to be healed. I told the paramedic that this is what I'm going to do, he said "ok."

I did, and I told him that he would be ok and that he would be healed. My Dad looked at me through one eye, with his face expressing a control over his excruciating pain.

I met my mother at the hospital, her worry was evident in her body language, and the look on her face. She said, "I don't think he will make it" . I held her and told her that it will be ok. We both waited outside the triage room, until the doctor came out, and told us that he was stable.

A day or so went by and all the family came together to visit my Dad in hospital. He was wheeled into the family visiting area, where he was greeted by his 8 children, and 3 grandchildren. At this time, there was only 3 grandchildren.

He was glad to see us, and us him. He looked fragile, but we knew he was doing ok. Tears were shed at the relief of his recovery. There was a warm feeling of love in the room as we are were lucky enough to all have been brought up with love for each other.

My Dad asked me to give him a blessing. That's what we did in our religion, we believe in healing by the laying on of hands, much like reiki. We said a prayer, and I placed both of my hands on his head, the pert of the head where the crown chakra is located.

As I laid my hands on his head, the feeling came, it was very strong, it was like walking into a warm shower. I felt it start at the top of my head, going down my neck and shoulders and into my chest. I began to speak, and again, as I spoke, I noticed that my voice changed, it was soft, it didn't even seem like it was coming from my vocal cords in my throat, but rather deep inside somewhere. As I spoke I told my father that he would live to see his family multiply, and that they would spread all over the world. The feeling in the room was electric, thick with a feeling almost you could almost touch with your hands. Tears were shed as the emotions of love were felt so strong. The blessing came to an end and my Father made a speedy recovery.

As little as 7 years later, my Father saw his family multiply and multiply. My sisters who had desired to have children for years, all of sudden began to have babies. I myself began to have babies with my wife. All together he saw his family multiply from 3 grandchildren to 26 ! 26 grandchildren came to our family in as little as 6 years. What a miracle, what a wonderful blessing for my father to see this and what more, how did I know that this would happen? The truth behind it simply is, I didn't know. I just spoke the words that came to me when the feeling filled my body. I really don't even think that I even spoke the words, but the spirit or Universal Energy knew, and it told my father that it would happen.

It really did. It happened alright. The question now is, does the Universal Energy, or God or the spirit of God or whatever you decide you believe, know the future?

Omnipresent means present everywhere. Omnipotent means all powerful and Omniscient means knows everything. Could this feeling or the Universal Energy be these three things? Well energy is everywhere, it's all around us, is it all powerful? It could be, it can cause the blind to see and raise people from the dead, does it know everything? The future past and present? Well, I found that out for sure.

CHAPTER 6

The months past, and during this time, I was mostly happy, everything was going well. One New Year's Eve, I drove to London for a new year's party.

It was there that I met a woman that I was to marry. She had long blonde hair, and seen to be popular with the boys. All the guys wanted to be with her, at the end of the party I approached her and asked her for her number. She didn't understand my Welsh accent, so I had to ask again. She gave me her number and we began messaging and calling each other. She lived in Yorkshire which was a 5-hour drive from where I was in Wales. I drove to see her every weekend. She was adamant that she didn't want a relationship, but I persisted. However there came a time when I said to myself ok, and backed off, I remember she called me and said that she would come to Wales, I said "ok," she said, "but not as friends, as your fiancé." I was shocked and drove up to see her, I took a ring and asked her to marry me. This was only 2 months after we had met. We set a date to be married in July, which was only 6 months after we had met. Needless to say this was too fast. We married and bought a little 1-bedroom miners' cottage, she was 20 years old and I was 23. Within the first few months it was very difficult, we were only now getting to know each other. We argued, she gave me the silent treatment, which by the way ladies is the absolute worst thing for a man, just yell at him or slap him or anything, but please the silent treatment is pure torture for us men. She fell pregnant, and I was very happy. I have always wanted to be a father, we actually got on pretty well when she was pregnant. We were relatively hard up for money, all my wages mostly went on bills, and my wife didn't work. It was time for the baby to arrive, but he was 2 weeks late and my wife went in to be induced. The labour was horrific, lasting nearly 30 hours, finally he was born, a whopping 10lbs 2oz baby boy ! I immediately knew his name. What a wonderful time it was, to bring a newborn baby home.

If you go into a house with a newborn baby there, pause for a moment and be still. Be open to the feelings in the home. You will find that there is a peace, a stillness and feeling of joy. A baby truly is a miraculous thing you know. The power to create a living thing truly is a God given gift, a wonder, and a blessing. I always look back and think I was too hard on my first boy, I really don't know why, maybe I was too young. I have regrets and wish I had that time again. He was a stubborn little lad and would never give up crying or nagging until he got what he wanted, which is a very good thing, that we now teach ourselves "never give up until you get what you want" so it was a wonderful gift he had. He still has it now an knows perfectly how to play it.

My wife and I still argued from time to time, and I would get fed up of the silly childish behaviour she would show. She would use always tell me that I didn't love her and appreciate her etc… even though I did. Maybe I didn't know how to show her, but I did. I would just get fed up of her emotional pulling and pushing, and I would call her out on it and tell her I wouldn't put up with it. I felt like she would always drag her heels in every direction I wanted to take the family. In hindsight, I should of let go and seen were she wanted to go, I was a stubborn, prideful man who thought he knew what to do and how life should be. One time I asked her to get into the car, she went into the back seat, and asked where are we going? I told her I was taking her back to her Mam and Dad. Silence followed for the 5-hour drive, well I ended up taking her back to wales and we tried again. Boy o boy I was a very proud and stubborn young man. I thought that I was doing my best and she should support what I was trying to do. I now know that's not a relationship I just didn't know any better, and I am sorry for how I was.

I valued the time I had with my first son, he was truly a magnificent young boy, always happy and enjoying our full attention. Oh how I loved him, he was my first-born son, my boy, and such a delight.

MORE THAN JUST A FEELING

18 months went by, and we found out that baby number 2 was on its way, pregnant again.

We had another beautiful baby boy ! 2 boys ! Oh what a joy ! I knew right away that this one had something special. He had a desire, he had a determination to succeed. Again the newborn baby feeling entered into the home, a peaceful time, a time of love and joy. I worked and my wife stayed at home, and looked after the babies. My second boy had a temper, when he was tired he would let you know ! He was the only boy to ever have had the courage to smack me right in the face ! It was out of pure frustration. Oh what a boy, such a delight.

Again time went on, my wife and I got on a little better, but still we had our moments. I still worked in the barber shop, and was happy working with my family.

I started to feel that I needed to earn more money in order to support my family, and I struggled with wanting to stay and support the family business and leave to earn more money. I didn't know what I would do as a job, but I knew I needed to do something.

It was during this time that my younger brother had married his childhood sweetheart. He had always loved her, they married and moved into a house together. He was to find out that she was not the girl he thought she was, and the marriage ended pretty soon after.

BY N.D.H

My brother was distraught, his world as he knew it, or how he thought he wanted it had ended, to make it worse she was pregnant. His mind was in turmoil, and I could see he was struggling with it. One day after a long hard day at the barbershop, he was pulling down the shutters of the shop as I walked to my car, and he said "goodbye" I said "goodbye" and walked on. As I drove home I had a feeling that there was something wrong, it came stronger and stronger. When I got home, I turned the car around and drove to my parents where he was living due to the separation. I called my older brother and asked him if my younger brother was there, he said "yes he has gone to bed to lay down", I asked him to go and check on him, he said "he was asleep". I knew, I really knew that he had done something, so I asked my older brother to check for any tablets laying around. He checked and found empty packets of sleeping tablets in the draw next to his bed. I told my brother to call an ambulance right away and that I'll be there in just a Minuit. I pulled up outside and ran in. I ran upstairs and jumped on my younger brother, I shook him to try and wake him, but he was out for the count, there was no waking him. I slapped his face to try and wake him but nothing. Finally the ambulance came, and took him into hospital, they said there is nothing much they can do except see how he comes around. They said this kind of sleeping tablets are for my older brother who suffers from mental illness, they are designed so that you can't really overdose on them. So my little brother had the best sleep of his life, he slept for about 2-3 days. He came around and regained his determination to carry on again. I can't help but think that he must have been in a really bad place to have had the actual courage and determination to want to leave this place. To fall asleep and never wake back up.

Life went on again for a few months, and things seemed to settle.

CHAPTER 7

Now it's time to tell you about my Nephew. My Nephew was born when I was about 5 years old, so in reality he was like a little brother. I remember going to see him and my oldest sister in the hospital shortly after he was born. My eyes were at the same level as the plastic crib he was laid in, so I could see his face. He was massive! 11lb born! He seemed to fill the plastic crib he was laying in, an exciting time, the first grandchild for my parents.

My Nephew had a skill, he would read, read, and read. By the age of 6 he had read Stephen Kings IT, that's a big book and scary for a 6-year-old. He was always a gentle soul, and still is to this day. He is 6ft 6, and around 120kg, and speaks with a very deep masterful voice.

Growing up we treated him just like our little brother and would tease him, one time when visitors were over, and my parents were entertaining in the living room. My younger brother and I stripped him naked and threw him into the room. My mother screamed and chased us up the stairs slapping at any part of us she could reach.

In the valleys of Wales, drugs is a huge social problem and its widely available to all, as you probably have guessed from my experience. At the age of 15, my nephew got involved with the wrong crowd, a very Wrong crowd, the crowd from the rough estates and they took drugs often. One day the police knocked on the door, and said that they had arrested my nephew for 3 accounts of armed robbery! We couldn't believe it, it turns out he held up 3 grocery stores, with the very same WW2 Banet that my older brother tried to stab himself with. The court case came, and he was sentenced to 3 years imprisonment. I remember, the day before the court case and knowing that he would do time. I took him into a private room and told him I loved him and that he should be brave, be strong and keep his head down, so he could get out early on good behaviour. We shed a tear at the thought of the life experience he would about to embark upon.

After his sentence I visited as often as I could with his mother and little sister.

On the day of his release, I went to pick him up with my sister. I can still see his face and large stature walking through the gates to freedom.

Some months passed, and I noticed that he was getting involved in the very same crowd that he got in trouble with.

I didn't know what to do, I tried to tell him that he would get in trouble again and go right back to jail if he carried on.

BY N.D.H

At this time I was still involved in the religion, and it was normal practice to go out and visit people. So one day my Dad and I had to pick who we should go and see. We both sat in the car thinking of who we should visit. I said to my Dad, "why don't we go and visit my nephew," so we did.

We went to my sister's house, and knocked the door. We were both dressed in suits, and she knew we were supposed to go out and visit people, but we went to see her and my nephew. It may have seemed that we were just wasting time and going to sit at hers while we were supposed to visit other people.

My nephew was there, we set the environment, by saying a prayer. I spoke to my nephew, and told him again that if he carries on this way he will go back to jail, and that he needed to change. He needed to change, I told him of my experience when I wanted to change, and hugged him and said goodbye to them, and told them we would see them for a family dinner later in the week.

That night, my nephew told me, that his desire to make a change in his life played on his mind most of the night, and then he took himself to his bedroom. There he knelt and offered his heartfelt desire to change to the Universal Energy. He then told me, that as he was praying and exerting his desires to the Universal Energy, the whole room filled with light. He didn't have the lights on, and it was the middle of the night, but the room filled with light. He said he could see it, and he could feel it. I understood immediately as I too had seen this same light during my mission in Scotland. We both were amazed and talked about how it felt and where it came from.

From that day onwards, my nephew, who had no qualifications, and followed mine and my younger brothers' example of leaving schooling at 14-15 years of age, began to study.

He locked himself in his bedroom and read. He undertook an open university degree in English Literature. He never went out, and stopped hanging around with the crowd he was getting in trouble with. A few years passed and he was still committed to his study, and read and read and read. He finally gained a degree from the open university in English literature. WOW, what a change, his skill, his talent, his passion for reading was put to use, and he gained a degree. But this was not all, he was still thirsty for study, and he went on to complete a master's degree in English literature and social sciences. My nephew who left school at an early age, who went to jail for 3 years, had gained a master's degree. Again that's not all, he was still thirsty for study, and now at the age of 35, has gained a PHD in English literature and social sciences. This man, who seemed like he was going to have a life of going in and out of jail, had completely changed his path. This change came when the light came to him in his room that night we visited him.

Let's look at this for a moment. A young boy, who had just spent 2 years in jail, and on his release seemed like he would live a life of going in and out of jail, had a desire to change. He took that desire to his closet, his private space, and offered that desire up to the Universal Energy late at night. A light filled the room, he saw it, he felt it, and from that day his life blossomed.

How ? Why ?

Like we have discussed already, the Universal Energy knows all things. It knew my nephews' desires, and came to him and helped him. The Universal Energy is pure love and pure and perfect intelligence. It loves us and wants to help us. It wants us to be happy and successful, it wants us to do good things, it wants us to help others by loving them and encouraging them, to lift up the heavy hearted, to reach out and lift up the chins of those whose heads are down with discouragement. Let us all, take this approach, let's go out and be kind, be loving and help the heavy hearted. You never will know what can happen.

CHAPTER 8

It's cold in Wales, and I loved a wood fired stove we had in our cottage. I loved the ambience it gave, the natural heat that emanated from it, the natural light of the flames.

Needless to say, with that kind of environment, baby number 3 was conceived! It seemed like just a few short months and my wife was in the hospital in labour. I remember going outside the room to speak to my Dad for just one second and a big scream came from the room. I rushed in, just Intime to see my 3rd boy being born. Again a whopping 10lb baby boy!

He was such a bundle of joy, again with a new personality, so serious at times, but now he is the joker of the family, so funny and carefree. A very sensitive soul, who cares for his family. He would always be the one who would give up his sweets to give to another, the one who would go without, so that others could have. Needless to say he was filled with a natural compassion for others. Plus, he had long blonde hair and blue eyes, just like his Dad. He would be in trouble with the girls for sure.

I needed a good supply of wood for the fire, and I

called a trees surgeon. I asked if he had any wood he could spare, he said "come and help yourself". I would make regular trips to his land and meet with him and his wife, fill up the car with wood and take it home. After a while I began to ask him about tree surgery, and I started to take an interest. I came to think that this could be the new career I had been thinking about. I decided to re-mortgage the cottage and start a business in tree surgery ! I bought a van and a few chainsaws, made leaflets, put ads in the paper, made business cards and really worked hard in trying to get some jobs. I quickly found that in a few short hours, I earned as much as I did in the barber shop all week. I got a taste for the money and really went to work. I started to get pretty busy cutting peoples trees down in their gardens. I never had earned so much money.

Then it came, my big break. I had a call from a company asking for 15 tree surgeons to travel to Hastings for one night's work. I didn't know what to do, but I said "yes ! I'll do it." I called everyone I knew, asking around for good lads that could cut trees down. I was up all night worrying about how I'm going to do this. But I did, I hired a bus, filled it with all the equipment and 15 lads. The night was a success and the business quickly grew from a one-man band to employing 15 people. Word spread that a young lad like me who had nothing, had won a 5-million-dollar contract. It was a rumour, and really that was all it was, but I decided to play along with it, I acted like I was, and I worked like I was.

There was a place I used to take the trees and wood chipping's, up on a hill with an abandoned house, it was called Captains Hill. For years I had a desire to build my own house. I had put it out there to the universe, and had even began drawing what it would look like. One day I was at captain's hill, the owner of the land asked me if I wanted to buy a piece of it, he had just gained planning permission to sell the land into 5 plots.

I said, "yes for sure !" I picked my plot and began to design my house. I drew it and drew it and designed it. I sent my sketches to an architect and he drew up working plans.

I had never built a house before, but from my days working construction I had an idea.

I hired an excavator and went to work levelling the plot and digging out the foundations. I had my brothers helping me. We poured the concrete, poured the slab and assembled the timber frame. Friends of mine were trade experts, and they helped with tiling the roof and facing the outer skin with bricks. It took 18 months for the house to be complete. During this time I was still contracting, cutting down trees for the railway, and for the power distribution companies, work was busy and so were the evenings. I was never at home, so imagine the surprise when my wife said she was pregnant again! We had another beautiful baby boy. My youngest of

4 wonderful boys, oh what a delight this baby was, so small. He is still so small, but so full of love and kindness. He suffered with eczema really bad, and I had to rub cream over his forehead arms and legs, the cream would sting for a moment and he would cry, I would hold him tight and rock him until the stinging went.

Wow, I had 4 boys under the age of 5. Bath time was fun, it was like a factory line. We moved into the house, a 6-bedroom 3 story house, it was massive ! Work was still good I was earning lots of money, money just kept coming and coming.

Then one day, well on my second son's birthday actually. We drove to a family dinner to celebrate. I noticed a scrupled-up piece of paper down in the drink holder in the driver's door. I don't know why, but I picked it up. My wife got out the car and I opened it. The words on the paper hit me like a wave of fire. I quickly scrupled it up and put it in my pocket. I gathered myself very quickly, and helped get the kids out of the car and ushered them into the venue. When the kids were all settled, I went to the bathroom and locked the door. I reached into my pocket and opened the paper once again to get a good look at what it really said. To my utter dismay, it was my wife's writing. It was a list of justifications to leave me for another man that she had met. She would always go to Yorkshire to visit her family, and it seemed that she had been seeing another man up there. I read the words "if he doesn't give me attention, I will find it in someone else" and " what about the boys" "how am going to tell my Husband."

Each individual sentence hit me in the stomach with so much force that I was sick. I was filled with a burning sensation that went right up to my ears and face. I was shaking.

Again I shook it off, and put the note back into my pocket, and went to join the rest of the family. I pretended that nothing had happened and carried on with the evening.

I didn't tell anyone about the note, and I kept it hidden for a few weeks. I watched my wife a little closer at what she was doing, who she was talking to, why she would go for a walk on her own. Then I started to look at her phone messages, I saw messages from a man that I knew, they were messages about how they could be together. Again the feeling of fire came up within me from my stomach to my face, and again I shook it off.

One day she was upset, and I asked her what was wrong? "Nothing she replied" then a few days later, I asked her if there was someone else? She looked at me right in the yes and said "No" I said, "are you sure?" she said, "No there is no one else." So I pulled the piece of paper out an presented it to her. Her eyes widened, and her mouth dropped, her face went pale and she admitted it. I asked "who?" She admitted that it was the man I knew from Yorkshire. She began to cry as did I. I tried to comfort her as we both sat on the bed. It was out, she knew that I knew.

The thing is, I never ever thought in a million years that something like this would happen to me. I thought my wife loved me, we had 4 wonderful baby boys, they were all still very young. I had just built a wonderful family home where they had a bedroom each. A playroom, a cinema room everything, business was going extremely well, and now this. I really did not know what to think or do. So I thought I would just wait and see. I knew that I could not trust her, and that I would never feel the same towards her. Maybe I was concentrating on work so much that she felt neglected, and that she did not have my attention. I really didn't know what to do. One night after work, we put the kids to bed and sat at the kitchen table, she said to me, "ok, I will have this house and you can go and live in a one bedroom flat somewhere?" Oh my goodness, I was astounded. I worked all day cutting trees, and all night and weekends on building this house for my family and she was going to turf me out to live in a one bedroom flat!

I said, "we should wait and see if we could work it out." A few weeks went by and I needed help. I needed to sell the house. I still had the little miner's cottage, so we could move back into that.

I remember it like yesterday, I was alone in an unfinished room, on an empty paint pot. I said a prayer. I asked if we would ever sell this house. It was in the middle of the financial crisis in 2008, and no one were buying houses. I really needed to sell the house and asked if we could. Then it came, the feeling, as I sat on the empty paint pot, with my head down and my shoulders slumped like a defeated man, the feeling came. This time no words or feeling of words, just the feeling from the tip of my head, down my neck and shoulders and into my body. I looked up as I knew that the Universal Energy was listening to my prayer, and that was it. The feeling came and then it went.

2 days later, there was a knock on the door. I opened the door and there standing in front of me, was a married couple on the porch. They introduced themselves, and then asked if they could buy the house. I could not believe it ! I said, "come in and have a look around." I showed them around and they loved it ! They made me an offer, I said "no" and told them what I needed, they agreed, and 8 weeks later the house was sold !

I began to upgrade the miner's cottage, and we moved back there. When we were settled I packed a black bin liner with my clothes and told my wife I'm going.

She was upset, I was upset the kids were upset, but I could not live with her, I did not trust her, I felt so let down and for me it was over.

The next few months were pretty tragic really if you think about it. I was a religious man, I had wonderful experiences with the Universal Energy, and I blocked it all out. I went AWOL if that's what you could call it. I drank, I smoked, I started to take cocaine, this was a daily habit. I took cocaine first thing in the morning to go to work. I worked, and came home and drank and slept with girls, and took cocaine, and smoked, and repeated this for a few months. I was out of control, so I decided to buy a dog. I always wanted a bullmastiff, but my wife wouldn't let me, so I did it. I bought a beautiful red bullmastiff girl I called her Bella. I would still have the children over on weekends, and we had so much fun. They would all sleep in my bed, 4 kids and me, it was wonderful. I decorated the house, and bought furniture, and was feeling like I was getting settled. But I knew inside that something was missing, I was missing something. Although I was living a lifestyle that many covet, drugs and rock and roll, I knew something was missing. It seemed that my "belly was full, but I was still hungry". Just like Bob Marley said.

One day I came home from work and took the dog for a walk. As I walked back I saw 2 men at my door. I knew that they were from the religion I belonged to, so I walked past, hoping they didn't see me. But they did, and knowing what it's like to be like them from my mission in Scotland, I gave in and went back and let them in. I put the dog in the kitchen, and offered the boys a drink. They sat down and started to talk to me, I asked them to talk about Jesus, and they

MORE THAN JUST A FEELING

did. I then said, "Can I tell you what I know of Jesus?" I began to tell them that I knew he walked on this earth, and that he was full of love and light. I told them that I knew he still existed, and that he knows who I am, and that he has rescued me. I knew it because I have felt the feeling tell me so. As I was telling these young men about of what I knew of Jesus. The feeling came and filled the room. It was electric but soft, warm and gentle. Tears came to my eyes, and I was filled with love. I knew then, that the love I was feeling was the Universal Energy letting me know that what I was saying was true. I thanked the boys for coming and they left.

Ok, so let us examine this again here. How can anyone gain a knowledge of something just through a feeling? I asked this question to another man who had felt the feeling. He asked me to open my hand and close my eyes, so I did. He reached his index finger forward, and rubbed it across the palm of my open hand. He said, "open your eyes," I did, and he asked me "what did I just do ?" I said, "you rubbed your finger across the palm of my hand," he said to me "how do you know ?" I said, "because I felt it !" "That's right" he said, "you felt it, you didn't see me do it, but you felt me do it, and thus you know that I did."

Wow, what a descriptive way to let anyone know, that they can know something just through feeling it. I thought and reflected on how I kept feeling the feeling, and by feeling the feeling I knew that there was an external energy force, or Universal Energy that existed. I had felt it. It comes out of nowhere, I don't try and feel it, it just comes, sometimes stronger at times than others, but I know exactly how it feels. The only time that I can say that I have seen it, was the time on my mission when I saw the light above our heads, and that a portion of it came down and entered into my chest. That's the only time I have seen it. All the other times I had felt it, but I knew it was there, I knew it because I had felt it.

Ok, so where was I, yes that's it, the missionaries went, and I carried on living how I was living. Having my kids on the weekend, and drinking and smoking, and taking cocaine and sleeping with girls when the kids were not there.

Christmas came, and my wife invited me over for Christmas dinner, I said "ok that would be nice." Christmas Eve came and I brought the children's presents over to hers. The kids were in bed, and she was looking good. She had subsequently raided our savings and had breast surgery, so she had a nice-looking figure. Things got a bit hot, and I missed her, we kissed and made love on the sofa, Infront of the fire. Yes the fire, it's the fire I tell you, it sets an ambience, an ambience of romance.

I left and came back in the morning. The kids came down the stairs and we opened the presents like we had always done. The kids loved it and were so excited and happy, I felt like I was home again. My wife made breakfast and cooked dinner as I played with the kids. After Christmas dinner, I fell asleep on the sofa, I felt comfortable to do so, and it was amazing. This is what I was missing, the home feeling, the fire was on, the kids were playing, we had a great dinner, and the feeling in the home felt so good.

At the end of the evening my wife and I talked, and we said we should give it another go, so we did. I moved back into the miner's cottage, and we slept in the same bed. The kids woke up in the morning, and we were both in the same bed together. I could see their beautiful eyes glisten with delight that Mammy and Daddy were back together.

My wife had gained a boyfriend during the time we were apart, his name was the same as mine. She broke up with him and I can tell that he was upset. He kept calling and calling, until finally I answered the phone to him and told him that he would need to go and stop calling. He didn't respond and just hung up. We never heard from him again, but he sent messages telling her that he would tell me everything. This shook my wife and she asked me to block him from social media. Probably so I didn't find out something that she didn't want me to know?

My wife quizzed me on the things I got up to when we were separated. I opened up and told her the whole truth. At hearing the truth, she was understandably upset, and we had another big argument. I said, "we weren't together," but she didn't want to know. So I said "ok, if we are going to do this and try again you're going to need to overcome it, or we can't go on as she will resent me for the rest of our lives. That's not a good start to trying again."

She said she would try. I obviously knew that she had been sleeping with her new boyfriend, but again, the focus was on me and the things that I did. The things he did with her sort of vanished. During this time of making up, we went away, for a weekend and made love and tried to come back together. We took the children to Yorkshire for a week to visit her family, and she found out she was pregnant again.

CHAPTER 9

We packed up everything, I folded the business and sold all the machinery and tools, and we went to live in Yorkshire on a beautiful idyllic farm. It was beautiful. A fresh start for us and the children. I had no work and no job and only enough money to live on for a few months.

After we lived there for a few months, my wife and I still didn't see eye to eye. The silent treatment persisted, and the emotional blackmail and abuse continued. But, now she was armed with extra ammunition. I had slept around whilst we were separated, this only gave her more emotional abuse to throw at me. I knew things wouldn't change and this is the only time in my life that I really contemplated killing myself. Thoughts would run through my mind like, well I've done all I can to try get the family together again, my wife will never change, she will always use emotional abuse to manipulate me and make me feel bad.

My life was on top! I had a successful company and a massive 6-bedroomd house. And now I'm living in a farmhouse in the middle of nowhere. I couldn't see a way forward. I would look at the barn opposite the house, horses stabled there, and I would even go in and look at where I could hang myself.

Then I would walk back into the house and see my beautiful children. Full of happiness and joy, a pure picture of delight, my little darling boys running around and playing.

Needless to say the thoughts of suicide left as I looked at these little angels, and the thought of another baby on the way.

We had only been in Yorkshire for a few months, and I had been asked to go back to Wales to attend something that is called a disciplinary council. The religion that I belonged to knew about my antics. And due to the status or level of responsibility I had been given within the religion, I needed to undergo questioning by the leaders of the religion in Wales.

I drove to Wales, and sat Infront of a council of 15 men. By my side was my good friend, he didn't need to be there, but he was there. I loved him, he had taught me so much about leading, talking and how to interact with people, but mostly how to serve people. What a jolly and spiritual man he was.

As I sat there, the president of the leaders, addressed me, and read out my confession.

This consisted of all the offences that I had made, and the promises I had broken. All the men in the room were quite as he read my confession out, all eyes were upon me. I confirmed the confession, and I answered questions that were asked with sincere honesty. I hid nothing, because I believed that the truth is the truth, and there is no hiding from the truth, so I opened up and confirmed everything, it was quite detailed to.

The last thing I said before leaving the room before a decision of discipline was made, was this. " My brothers, I have sat where you are now sitting, and I know of the rules and regulations and standards of this religion. If any of you feel that you want to be kind, caring and try and let me off lightly. I would ask you not to. I know the decision that you need to make, and if you love me like you say you do, you would pass the most severe judgement you can" Which meant that I would be excommunicated from the religion.

I thanked them and left the room to await the decision.

On return, the judgement was passed, and I received it. I was excommunicated form the religion that I had been brought up within.

Immediately I felt a huge weight lift from my shoulders, and I felt happy. A strange feeling to have at this time, but I really did feel happy.

I left and drove back up to Yorkshire to be with my children.

How life can change so much?

In a matter of a few months I had gone from having a wealth of material items, and holding a high office within the religion. To having no material items and being excommunicated from the religion.

A total 180 degree turn in my life. I really struggled to understand why, it played on me how this had happened so fast. I began to question everything I thought I knew. I believed that God or the Universal Energy knew that this would happen to my life, as we have already said, that it is Omniscient and knows the future the past and the present. So if God knows the future, he knew that this would happen to me. This was a bit of an eye opener and a new concept to me. It was a time of surrender and acceptance of everything that had happened. I had to trust that the Universal Energy knew the future, and knew that this was going to happen to me in my life.

I knew that change is the only constant in life, and that life will always change. A story of a gardener came to me, the story goes something like this.

There was a beautiful glorious rose bush. This rose bush was tall and blossomed beautiful rose's, it was happy and delighted in the progress it had made in becoming a beautiful rose bush. Then one day the gardener came and saw the rose bush. The gardener appreciated the beauty of the bush, and loved the rose bush beyond comprehension.

Then the gardener took out his shears and clipped the rose bush right down to the ground, cutting all of its branches and flowers off. All the growth and beauty of the bush had been taken, cut off, and all that remained was what looked like an empty stalk and a few empty twigs.

The rose bush cried and cried and cried, and said to the Gardner, "Why? Why have you come and done this to me? I was doing so well. My flowers were bright and beautiful, I was big and tall, and was pleasing to your eye, you loved me, and you say you love me beyond my comprehension, and you have come and stripped all my beauty you have cut me down to the ground. I don't understand why you have done this, it hurts. The physical pain of being cut, and now the emotional pain of trying to understand why, please gardener, why have you done this to me?"

To which the gardener responded " My beautiful wonderful rose bush, I do love you beyond your own comprehension. I have watched you and have seen you grow from a seedling. I have appreciated your beauty and have smelt the flowers that you have given. But my wonderful rose bush, I see what you do not see, and I know what you do not know. I know ,that by cutting you down, and trimming your branches, really is the best thing for you. You will grow stronger, stronger than you were before, giving off more beautiful flowers than you have done before. By doing this to you, you will become an even better rose bush than you were before. Trust me and believe in me"

As all rose gardeners know, Rose bushes need cutting right down, right back at the end of every growing season in order for them to produce better the following season.

So if any of you feel that you have been cut down, please take courage. Have courage that it is for your own benefit. You will grow again and become better for it.

Know that you are loved and that all of life's events are controlled by the Universal Energy.

We can learn faster, by trying to surrender and accept what has happened. We can overcome the tragedy by accepting it and trying to learn from it. Tools to help you, that helped me. Are, Prayer, yes everyone says it, but its true, prayer is key, so is mediation, anything that can help you get in touch with the Universal Energy. Energy is light and where there is light there can be no darkness remember.

So when we try and have access to the Universal Energy, it can help us heal faster, help us understand, help us surrender and help us accept what has happened to us.

For any living thing to grow, we need nourishment! What nourishes living things? The soil does, nutrients from the soil. Water, they need water to drink otherwise they dry up and die, and of course light, light is needed for growth.

So ok, what can we relate this to? Soil – Water and Light.

MORE THAN JUST A FEELING

Soil can be seen as Truth.

Water can be seen as Faith and Hope

Light can be seen as Love.

What is truth ? Truth is truth right, how do we know what truth is ? Many religions fight and argue over what is true, and what is not. But we can learn our own truth. Scientist tell us what they think is true by years of research, and they tell us that this is the fact. Only to learn and discover years later, well actually, this is what we thought was true, but we now know that this is true and that was not. Can we rely of scientific truth ? Some yes, some no, because we as humans are not yet perfect and are always learning.

Truth to me is a little of both. There can be only one truth, and to be completely honest I'm still learning what the truth is. All I know is what I now know at this moment in time, of the truth that I believe is true. A lie is a lie, deceit is deceit, love is love and light is light.

I know what love feels like, to me. And I know that light disperses darkness.

I know that we are not perfect, and I know that we can continually progress towards perfectness. Perfectness where all knowledge of truth is gained. Therefore do we not rely on someone else's truth. Religious script, and teachings? Personal experiences? And teachings of great spiritual leaders? Gurus?

BY N.D.H

One day I was working, asking permission to cut tress down under the powerlines and I knocked a door. An old man came to the door, I asked if we could cut these trees back from the powerlines coming to this house, and if he could sign the permission docket. He signed DR so and so…. DR… oh I asked, "you're a doctor," he said, "yes I am," I asked, "Dr of what if a may ask," he said, "a doctor of phycology." "Oh" I said, "that's interesting, please Dr, may I have a chat with you?" He obliged and we sat at his table, I said "Dr, you're an old man, and have been a Dr of phycology all your life, what can you tell me from all your years of experience on this earth and all your studies, about how I'm feeling." I described about my confusion in religious beliefs and how my life had seemed to crumble. He said 2 things to me, that have stuck with me and will never leave me.

He said this

1- "Why don't you go around and study all the religions, and take from them what you feel is good and true, and build your own truth, it will be your own truth and you can decide what you want to take from the religions and what you don't, the same with spiritual leaders, take from them what feels good and leave what you don't think is good, build your own truth."

2- He said "my boy, look at my garden, if I did not go out there and cut back those tress and ivy and grass and all the vegetation, it would engulf my home, all the vegetation would consume my home, so in your life, continuously trim back the vegetation be a gardeners of your own mind, you are not a victim of your circumstances, you are not a victim of your environment. You can continuously improve your circumstance, and change your environment by trimming back the vegetation. That takes work, and work is action."

I really believe that I was supposed to meet this DR, what sound advice he gave. If your searching for truth, go around and learn as much as you can and take what you believe and leave what you don't, and make your own mind up. Build your own truth. But how do you know if what you like is truth or not? I'll tell you what I do, but it's what I do, and what I believe, you don't have to agree, I'm just telling you what I do to believe the truth I believe.

When presented with any teaching of any kind, I look at it. I study it a little, and I have a go at it, then I pray and meditate upon it. I try and get In Touch with the Universal Energy and ask the Universal Energy "is this true ? it feels good when I think about it and when I practice it I feel good inside but I want to be sure, so please God let me know if this is true."

When I do this sincerely, if the thing I believe to be true is true, I have the feeling. The same feeling that I have had through my life, from a young boy. The feeling that is like standing under a warm shower starts at the tip of my head, goes down my neck and shoulders and into my chest, a warm and comforting feeling. Sometimes it makes me quiver and shake.

Then I accept it as truth, my truth. When I don't get that feeling, if it just doesn't come, I am left with feelings of confusion doubt and frustration. Then after a while I accept that it can't be truth, my truth. And I let it go. Sometimes letting it go is hard because you really like it and want it to be true, and have it as your truth. Anyway, that's how I do it. You can try it if you like, it may or may not work for you. But that's what I do.

What is Faith and Hope ? is it the same thing or not ?

To me, faith is an action word. "Faith without Works is Dead" so when I have faith in something I work at it. For example, a man sitting on his roof in a major flood. He prayed for help and truly has hope that he will be saved. He is really believing in his hope that he will be saved. A helicopter comes along and says, "come let's go, here is the ladder climb up." He shouts back and "says nah man, its ok I'm going to be saved, I'll just sit here and be saved." Then the helicopter goes, and the man sits there and wonders why he isn't being saved. Faith to me, is grabbing the bloody ladder and climbing it to the top, and into the helicopter. To me Faith is Work. It's an action word. If you have faith in something you will work for it. If we do this, then this is what all the mind over matter people teach. Really really believe it, think about it all day and all night, and focus all your attention on it. But get off your ass and work for it. It just will not appear because you think about it and focus it in your mind. To do something, we need to do something.

What is light or love?

To me again, and all this is just my outlook on things. You can make your own minds up as your truth may be different from my truth, and that's perfectly ok and wonderful.

To me light is love, a pure love. Love replaces darkness, darkness flees at the first ray of light, like the sunrise after a dark night.

Now, in a physical sense, darkness is good if you're an owl, or any nocturnal animal. It's what they were created to be in, they have been designed that way. But we humans have not, and darkness is uncomfortable for us. We can't see, we are afraid because we have panic receptors that make us paranoid. If we can't see any perceived threat, we need to feel safe. Early humans would lock themselves in a makeshift hut or cave in order to keep safe from nocturnal hunting animals. We lit fires to see in the dark, like we do now, we have the lightbulb which lights up the darkness, to make us feel a bit more secure.

Have you ever, had a long hard night physically, and

or emotionally? I have had both, I'm sure you could think of a few yourself. I would climb tress full of ivy in the dark with little light, it was hard to see and dangerous. When the sunrise broke, how much more comfortable I felt. I could see, and I knew my rope was in a safe place. I could see branches landing all around, I could see the danger and mitigate it.

Spiritually, Light is similar. It helps us see more clearly. Darkness inside, can be related to fear, doubt, worry, emotional pain and turmoil.

When the light comes, inside, it disperses all those negative feelings. Where there is light, there can be no darkness. I know this as my truth, because of the experience I had with light. Remember I saw it come down and enter into my chest, then I was happy, and I felt good. Light is more powerful that darkness my friends.

What about Love?

There are a few physical differences in love. The Greeks have words for each type of love, Agape – Selfless love, - Eros – Romantic love, etc.

Love is something so deep that it is hard to explain. It comforts, sooths, and uplifts.

Some people say that love hurts, but Liam Nelson said that love doesn't hurt it's the only thing that doesn't. Disappointment hurts, betrayal of loyalty hurts, but love, love doesn't hurt.

We can love others by loving ourselves. When we

open our hearts, we look at people differently, we see them as energy. Energy that has potential. Mrs Hinkley said that *if we could read anyone's life book, we wouldn't be able to not love them.*

CS Lewis said that *if we could recognise who we were. We would realise that we were walking with possible Gods and Goddesses whom, if we could see them in all their eternal dignity and glory, we would be tempted to fall down and worship.*

Wow, what a statement, this brings me back to the potential progress of all energy to its perfect state.

We can begin to love when we open our hearts. And by doing so we can heal ourselves and help others to heal also. When we say we should love others, Ram Das, said *we need to be careful that we don't collect lovers.* Just because we love everyone, does not mean that we collect lovers. Remember now, there are different types of love, and we should not confuse them. God Love is when we can love all things in a pure way. Romanic love is the love where we open our hearts to an individual in a romantic love, we embrace them physically and emotionally, we give ourselves, our bodies to each other. In the God love we do not. Because, love is so powerful we need to understand that there are bounds to which it is governed. If we love everyone in a romantic love we would collect lovers all over the town and be sleeping with everyone catching diseases and getting everyone pregnant this is out of control. So the confusion between loving everyone without bounds or limits or controls needs to be looked at, otherwise families wouldn't exist, just uncontrolled procreation.

Tell me you understand this ...

Where does love come from ?

Loves comes from God, or the Universal Energy, that energy is within us. It comes to us, it resides in us. It is light.

You know, that man makes bombs. Super powerful bombs, and has always looked for outside chemical reactions to make the biggest bomb they could. But it wasn't until someone looked inside, by splitting an atom. That the most powerful bomb ever has been made.

When we look outside, we see an endless universe. When we look inside we can see the same. It is from the inside the most amazing chemical reaction is made. The sperm meeting the egg, life is created. Creating life is a God like Gift. Can you make life by carving a piece of would and sprinkling a bit of dust over it? If you said yes, I would say your like Pinocchio and your nose is growing.

Love is all encompassing there really is no greater thing than love.

Jesus said to *love one another as I have loved you*, and that we should *love thy neighbour as thyself*, and the bible said that *there is no greater love than this, that you lay down your life for your brother.*

Think upon this, and think about what love means to you, and let's try and love everyone and everything.

CHAPTER 10

Life went on in Yorkshire, my wife and I tried and tried and tried but I knew that she was struggling to accept my behaviour whilst separated. It was always there, lurking in the back round a dirty sticky subject that I tried to always avoid talking about. But it always managed to rear its ugly head, and she wouldn't let me forget it, I have never cheated on my wife whilst we were together, not even one kiss. Never mind it was what it was, and as you will see in the coming chapters, my wife couldn't ever let it go.

I worked for a few companies cutting trees and surveying trees, for a while, but my heart wasn't in it, and I left. I decided that I would go to university and study civil engineering ! Now for a man that had very little schooling leaving school at the age of 14/15, with no qualifications at all, this was a daunting task. I went to the open day and inquired about what courses I should do. I talked to the lecturers there, and told them I had no qualifications, but wanted to complete a degree in civil engineering. They looked at me suspiciously, but I was serious. I had a goal in mind, and I was determined to do my very best in attaining this goal. It was my last attempt of making this family work. I love my children and want the best for them, so I made a plan. A plan of how to emigrate to Australia!

I could of gone on a temporary visa cutting trees, but the thought of cutting trees in Australia in 30- 40 degrees was not very attractive at all. So I thought that after building my house I could build anything, and if I wanted to build I would need the civil engineering qualification.

On the university open day, I remember talking to a little Irish man. It would have been his decision if I would be excepted onto the course. I explained my desire, and he told me that I needed to complete a subsidiary course designed around civil engineering. It was a 2-year course part time, and that I would need to get distinctions in every subject, in order to be excepted onto the civil engineering course. Challenge excepted!

What was I doing ! I had no idea about what I was getting myself into. I didn't even know how to use a computer. I didn't know how to open a word document, never mind how to organise and present an assignment. The first day of my new adventure came. I was very nervous. I bought pens and pencils, a bag, a calculator, and everything I thought I would need, it was like my first day at school. I was 34 ! I walked into the class, and the students went quiet. I sat at the front, all the young student kept looking at me, and were quiet. I went red, and didn't know what to do, so I looked at them and nodded my head politely. They all thought that I was the new lecturer! They didn't think I was another student until the real lecturer walked in and began to take the class.

So that was funny. The lecturer asked us to take a computer and open a word document. I turned the computer on and didn't know what else to do, so I asked the young student next to me if he could show me how to do it, he smiled and said "ok man, you click this and double click on that and there you go." "Thank you" I said and put my glasses on and eagerly looked at the computer. The teacher asked us to write a report on a certain subject, I can't remember which now, but as he walked around the class to look at the students' progress I was nervous. He was getting closer to me, and I really didn't know what to do. I wrote a heading, made it bold, and underlined it in aerial 12 font.

Ok I was going to get into it, I wiggled my fingers and began typing away. The lecturer came closer looking at the students' progress. He had a slow steady walk nodding approvingly at the students work. And then he came to me. He stopped talking to the class, and stopped behind me. I didn't look at him, I just went for it typing with one finger. I knew he was behind me, he wasn't moving and wasn't speaking. I went red, and was not going to give up. I was tapping away with my one finger, circling it over the keyboard until I found the letter I needed. Then, he put his hand on my shoulder, I looked around expecting a frown of disapproval just like I had received from the teachers at school. But this was not the case. I remember, when I turned to look at him, he was smiling with a face of encouragement. "Keep going" he said, "keep going."

My first assignment was terrible, a finger tapped letter with a few headings. But I had one thing, one little advantage over the other students. I had worked construction, and had seen the practises that were being taught, so I knew exactly how to describe the practice and the methods, and what they were for and how to use them. I knew because I had seen and used the process in real life. Although the other student were computer wizzes, I had only one advantage, life experience.

From that day on I wasn't nervous one bit. I went gung hoe, I caught the bus into the city, and went to my new school with a happy enthusiastic smile, soaking up everything that was being taught. I struck an unwritten deal with my fellow students. I would tell them about the process, and what this was for, and what that was for. And they would help me with my computer work. It worked very well, and we had a great class. All my classes were great ! Except one. Maths Class ! Oh my goodness, you know I can use a calculator to add and take away a divide and multiply but man, that's it. When the teacher started to draw, X's and Y's on the board and said "find the value of Y," I almost laughed, I said to myself "you cannot be serious, how can you find the value of Y when it's a Y, it's not even a number."

So I that was my introduction to algebra. I was later introduced to calculus, and let me tell you, when you can wind something up, and wind it back down again using nothing but numbers, you must be a magician. I attempted the first homework in readiness for the first assignment, and oh no, it was horrible, it was presented terribly, the answers were all wrong. And when it was marked, the teacher took me outside and said never hand this work in again.

So I needed to get top marks in each subject, a distinction, which is the highest mark, and how I was going to get that in maths I really didn't know. I wondered what I could do. And like a spark of inspiration, I got a maths tutor ! 2 nights a week. I went to a maths tutor and she taught me the basics of algebra and calculus and formulas and problem solving. She was amazing, a very sweet lady so kind. I would go 2 nights a week for the remaining five years of my studies. And without her, I would never of past my first assignment.

The maths teacher was always suspicious about me. She wasn't very empathic. A large lady with thick glasses. She looked at me and would ask me questions in the class that I couldn't answer. But my assignments came back with the correct answers. I had it down ! see, where there is a will there is always a way.

I was getting distinctions in all my assignments, I was learning and learning, I was loving it. I enjoyed my classmates, although they were all 10 years younger we were all mates, and we all got on well. Assignments came in, and I got them back in in record time. I would work on them the day they were handed out, and I was getting top marks in everything!

The end of the year came, I got distinctions in everything and I was accepted on to get the degree.

Whilst I couldn't really sustain a family of 5 on student loans and grants, I started to apply for every construction job I could. Nothing ever came back, I must of filled in hundreds of applications, for trainee this and trainee that, but nothing. It was disheartening, I needed a job. I had 5 children to support, time and time again I tried, but nothing.

Then one morning I went around the back of the house to smoke. I didn't want the kids to see me smoking, so that's where I went. I sat down on the step to smoke, and pondered and prayed about a job. I needed a job and I needed it to fit around my studies. It was almost an impossible task. As I was smoking and praying, it came, the feeling came. As it had many times in my life, but I had not felt it for a while. I thought that I wouldn't have the feeling again because I was not a part of the religion or anything. But sure enough it came, in the very same way it had before, from the top of my head down my neck and into my chest. This time it spoke, but not with words, no words, it said to me, "Today is the day." And I knew that it was the Universal Energy, it had been seeing me, and watching me and this time this very morning when I was smoking, it came and said to me "Today is the day."

In turned out that today was indeed the day. I had a call from an old friend that was a director of a large railway firm. I remember the first time we met, we met to price some vegetation clearance so he could carry out some embankment stabilisation works. He called me and offered me a job as a site manager, in Yorkshire about 20 mins from where I lived. Although the company was based in Scotland, and his office was over in Manchester 1.5 hours away. I went in for the interview I told him of my situation and that I was about to study full time towards a degree in civil engineering. He said he would support me in that, and give me the days off I needed to attend university. What a wonderful gift from the universe. How that all fell in place was a wonder to behold. I signed up as promised by the Uni lecturer, and decided that I would study full time, because I only needed to attend 2.5 days per week, and a full-time course would allow me to complete the degree in 3 years ! So I signed up, full time education, and a full-time job. It turned out to be a full-time job because the hours I was working were 40hours or more per week. On the railway a lot of work is carried out under track possessions, where they shut the track down, and this was mainly night-time. So

I worked and I worked, and I studied, and I studied. My job was going well, I was impressing the management and my studies were going well also. I was still getting distinctions in all subjects and I was getting paid well and getting my work done.

I would sometimes come straight from a night shift right into university and then go home, it was tiring but I loved it.

I Thought that homelife was going well to, but looking back my wife was pregnant and busy with the four boys. I just thought I was doing the right thing and I thought she was too. But It turned out differently than what I thought.

One day my wife called, and the baby was on its way ! We went to the hospital, and everything seemed to be going well, until the time came to push. As she was pushing the heartbeat of the baby was dropping. The consultant came in and carried out a few tests which involved scratching the baby's head with a scalpel, testing the blood for the oxygen levels. The tests failed a few times, and he had to do it again and again until I said, "hey man that's my baby your hurting, get her down to surgery and get this baby out safely". As they were prepping for surgery, one big push came, and the baby was out ! An absolutely beautiful baby girl. I immediately fell so in love with her, my baby girl had finally come, 4 boys and a baby girl. Oh how wonderful it was, the boys loved her, and spoiled her, and looked after her, and gave her everything she ever wanted. She quickly learnt that all she needed to do to get what she wanted was to scream. I loved her, and loved her. She was wonderful. She is 7 now, and has long blonde hair and walks around like a ray of sunshine. Laughing and joking and making people happy. Oh what a wonderful gift. It's totally different having a girl, she was delicate and lovely. Having a girl has soften me.

Now I had 5 children to house, clothe and feed, and was more determined than ever to succeed. Succeed in gaining a degree and emigrating to Australia to provide the best that life could offer for my family.

I worked and worked and studied and studied. As my wife started to gain confidence in her body again, she started to go out, which I didn't mind at all. She needed the break after looking after the kids all week. She started to go to the local pubs in the village. I think there were only 2, and she started to get a lot of attention from the local men too. Which I did mind. Sometimes she would go out and not come back in until 4am. I thought nothing of it and probably nothing ever happened. The men in the village would flirt with her, and she started to enjoy all the attention she was having. After all I had kept her pregnant for almost all of our married life. It started to get to me a bit, I was working all the hours I could, I was studying all the spare hours I had, and looking after the kids on weekends when she would go out. I wasn't happy and she knew it.

University was still going well, and I had a great team of lecturers they were fantastic, caring and really interested in making sure we all understood, so we could do our best in the assignments. I came into one lesson and the lecturer told me that she had entered me into a national award, I said "oh really ? ok" thinking nothing of it. However a few weeks later I walked into the same lesson and the same lecturer told me that I had won! I won the most outstanding adult learner of the year out of all of the UK. I had to go to the house of parliament to receive my award. I couldn't believe it, there I was in the first year, I couldn't even open a word document and 4 years later I was in the houses of parliament receiving a national award. They made a film about me and everything, I could not believe it. I had to give a speech at the evening dinner. I remember drinking a few vodkas before I went up. The room was full of CEOs from all the top tier construction companies in the UK. I went up and this is more or less what I said.

" Good evening ladies and gentlemen. I just want to express gratitude to my lectures and my fellow students for the help and support they gave me during my studies. I want to tell you 2 things. 2 things that will help anyone achieve anything they want. The first is, "that in which we persist in doing becomes easy, not that the nature of the thing has changed but our ability to accomplish it has increased." This is the second, "our doubts are indeed our traitors, that make us lose the good that we may often win by fearing to attempt", if we use these 2 things in our lives they will serve us just like tools. like a hammer and a chisel, and with them we can carve out our futures" and I went and sat down to a standing ovation. I really couldn't believe it, from no qualifications no education not even knowing how to work a computer to standing Infront of the CEOs of the top tier construction companies giving a speech. Life is good.

CHAPTER 11

I was finally awarded a degree, and student life had come to an end. A wonderful time in my life. Armed with the degree, I was now able to start an application for a permanent resident visa for emigration into Australia. I was so excited, the dream, the goal to take my lovely children to a wonderful land of sun, sand and surf. We saved and saved, we filled in paperwork and paperwork, my wife was right behind me, supporting me by filing in forms and getting all the information together. She was always very good at that.

We needed 60 points to get the visa we wanted. We had everything we needed, but I needed to carry out an English test, yes an English test. I needed to get top marks in order to gain the 20 points we needed to get the visa. I booked it and studied for it, and the day came for me to take the test. It was a computer-based test, it lasted for 3 hours! I thought I would get it first time, I spoke English for goodness sake, so how hard could it be, well it was hard ! it was very hard. There were essays to write, there was repeating sentences that you needed to memorise, there were short lectures that I needed to listen to and write about, and no spell check ! No red lines appeared under the text. I had to get all spelling and grammar correct, the test went on and I did my best. The results came through and I didn't get top marks. I only got just enough to gain 10 points, which was not enough, I needed 20 ! So I booked again, I said to myself "I'll do it again and again until I get the 20 points." The second test came, and I again did my best, the results came and nope, I only got enough for the 10 points, but I needed 20 ! so I booked again. This time I was determined, I asked all the family to pray for me, because we needed the 20 points, or we wouldn't get the visa. I remember driving to Sheffield, and pulling up in a car space near the test centre. This time I felt different, this time everyone was praying and hoping that I would get it. I said a prayer to myself in the car, and then it came, the feeling came, and it felt just as it did all the other times. I knew that this time was the time I would do it. The feeling was so assuring it felt like I was walking on air as I walked to the test centre.

I went in and tried my best, I looked at my spelling, checking the words, my full stops, and sentence forming and paragraphs and everything I could. The test had a timer, and you need to complete the test in time before it runs out. I finished the test in 3 hours, just less than the allocated time, and left. I had a little more confidence this time around, because I had the feeling, it hadn't come before when I did the other tests, but this time it did, and it has never let me down before.

I went back to work, and a few days later, the results came through. I was nervous opening the email, so I took a breath and opened it, yes! I had top marks in everything! Not one question wrong I completed it and gained the 20 points we needed to apply for the permanent visa we needed.

How does this happen? Why does it happen? The feeling came and I passed. The Universal Energy knew that I was taking the test, and that I needed to get 20 points to apply for the visa. The Universal Energy came to me at this time, the third time of taking the test, and it let me know that everything is going to be ok. By feeling this feeling, I knew that I was going to pass, and that's not all, by feeling this feeling I knew that I was meant to take my family to Australia. Otherwise why would I have passed, why would I have gained a degree, why did it all just fall into place and unfold before me. The feeling guided me to this point in my life. The feeling always came to help me, to let me know what I was doing was right. So I was so sure that by feeling this feeling my life was guided to go to Australia, it all just fell into place. Australia is where we should go for sure.

We gathered all the information and sent in the application for the visa. This was in the end of September. In record time the visa application came back, it came back in just 4 weeks, the end of October. We were all granted permanent residency in Australia, all the children my wife and myself, I just couldn't believe it.

We decided to make the move at the end of November, so we did. We sold everything! We packed 7 big suitcases and got on that plane. 5 children 7 suitcases, and $20,000 dollars in the bank. That's all we had. On the plane we were all excited, we were all nervous, but excited for our new life in Australia. Maybe this is just what we needed, a fresh new start in a new country. The children would live by the beach, the sun would be out, the weather would be amazing, the opportunities that Australia had to offer would be fantastic.

The morning of the flight came, we all packed up the suitcases into the van that came to pick us up. We said our goodbyes to family, and left for the airport. We needed to travel to Manchester, so we took the motorway. The M60, this was the highest motorway in the UK, and it was very cold. Snow started to fall when we were at the highest point, and at one point it started to fall very heavy. I didn't think we were going to make it to the airport in time. It was a struggle for the driver to see, never mind drive. But we soon came through it, and made the flight Intime. During the first flight, one of the boys began to complain of a stomach-ache and began to be violently sick. Every 2-3 minutes he was being sick, we were asking for sick bags all the time. Then one of the other boys started to be sick. 2 of them being violently sick. They had temperatures, and were not very well at all. Then the third boy started to be sick ,3 of them all being sick, sick everywhere, it was horrendous. I tried and to look after them, dabbing water over their heads to keep their temperature down, holding them to comfort them, getting sick bags from the air hostesses. Everyone was looking at us, the poor boys were so ill, a stomach bug for sure. What a time to get a stomach bug, on the plane, no room for anyone to lay down except on my lap. I had the three boys laying all over me trying to keep them cool and clean from all the sick. My wife sat Infront holding our baby girl. We changed flights in Dubai and whilst walking through the airport my other boy started being sick, and when he is sick he is sick. He made a massive noise, and threw up right on the floor Infront of him, in a busy airport. I could not believe it, all 4 boys being violently sick on the journey over to our new life. They were sick everywhere. Everyone was looking, but I didn't care, I was just trying to make sure the boys were ok, and we got to our connecting flight. We boarded the connecting flight and braced ourselves for the 14 hours long haul journey to our destination.

The children were still very ill, and we just did our best to get through it. The boys and I were covered in sick. We smelled, we were exhausted. The last few hours came, and 3 of the boys started to feel better. They were a lot more active and I could see that the bug had started to leave them. But my oldest was still ill, the flight landed, and we got off the plane and went through to immigration. I really could not believe how hard that flight was, the poor boys had a terrible time. We approached the immigration gate, and were in the front of a big que, about to hand over all our passports. Then yes, my oldest boy made a massive noise again, and threw up on the carpet right Infront of the desk. The immigration officer quickly scanned the passports and we went through. 5 kids 2 adults and 7 suitcases in Australia, violently sick all way over, but we made it. We were there. We came through the gate to be met by my brother. I threw my arms around him and cried. "We made it bro" I said, "we made it." 5 years in the planning, hard work and dedication, and a lot of miracles later ,and we had made it to Australia.

He took us to his home, we showered and cleaned ourselves up and rested, the children were so tired, as was I.

The following day, we all felt much better, and went to the holiday home that we had arranged to stay in for 4 weeks, until I found a job and could move into rented accommodation. The holiday home was on an island. We had to catch a ferry from the mainland to the island, 5 kids 2 adults and 7 suitcases. The time of the ferry was the school rush hour, so it was hectic. We managed to load all the children onto the ferry, and all 7 suitcases. People were looking at us, I don't know what they must have thought, but it surely was a sight to behold. We got to the island, and found the car that came with the holiday home at the carpark. We loaded the suitcase in ,and I drove with my oldest to the house, unloaded and went back to pick up the rest of the family. The car was overheating ! so we had to stop and let it cool down. There was a leak in the radiator, and we had to fill up the water, and hope that its wold get us back to the house, before it overheated again.

We finally all got into the house, and the kids were all excited, a new holiday house to explore.

It was warm that night, and we all woke up to the sound of birds screeching and crickets, it was a very strange environment to be in. we couldn't help but laugh.

That day, we saw our very first cockroach ! It scuttled across the floor in our bedroom, we all screamed and jumped around, we didn't know what to do, "a cockroach!" we all shouted. One of my boys isn't afraid of anything, and he quickly came to the rescue. He caught it in a glass cup and threw it outside, we all fell about laughing.

We needed to go food shopping, so we checked the car for the water level, and found that it was empty, so we filled it up, and filled up a bottle of water to take with us just in case. The rush to get to the shops before the car overheated was a tense moment. We completed the shop, checked the car and got back as quickly as we could. The car hissing and steaming at our arrival back the house.

BY N.D.H

That afternoon a storm broke, and the thunder and lightning was an amazing sight to see. We all stood out on the porch, watching this amazing show of nature, when suddenly the biggest crack of thunder clapped right above our house. It was just like a bomb had exploded, we all fell off our chairs and I shouted, "everybody in everybody in", and again when we all recovered from the shock, we fell about laughing. What were we all doing here? A family that had lived in the valleys of Wales and the dales of Yorkshire, had moved over the other side of the world in a strange country on a strange little island. We must have been crazy. But I knew deep down inside, that this is where we were meant to be. Otherwise why would the feeling had led us here. Why did I gain a degree, and why did I pass the immensely difficult English test? The feeling had guided us here and I was certain of it. I felt that everything would be ok. I trusted in the feeling with all my soul, and I knew that we were here because of its guidance.

A week or so passed, and we had been taking the children back and forth to the mainland almost every other day. We explored the island and knew our way around pretty well. We became familiar with the heat and the surroundings. The car was still overheating but we were prepared, always taking water with us to leave in the car, it became a little ritual, check the car for water, make sure we had water in the car to refill it if was emptying. Always watching the temperature gauge as we were driving back and forth to the shops or the ferry terminal.

It was so much fun, the children were having a wonderful time full of new adventures. However amidst all of this fun, in the back of my mind, I was a little concerned. We were spending money fast. I had been making enquiries for jobs, but nothing came back just yet, I was starting to get a little nervous. I started to get up at 5am every day and I sat on the porch to watch the sun rise, and I would say a prayer. I would offer my gratitude for the guidance of bringing us all here to this wonderful country, and I would ask that I would find a job. The heat of the morning sun would make me sweat as early as 5am in the morning. Coming from the snow and minus temperatures to 35 40 degrees on an island in Queensland, took a little bit of getting used to.

So this was my daily routine, I would get up and pray at 5am facing the sunrise. So that meant I was facing east.

Our savings had begun to get tighter and tighter as the days went on. I made calls every day to potential employers, but nothing was happening. I was really getting nervous. We had 1 week left in this holiday house that we rented for just one month. I was down to the last $5000, 5 children, 2 adults, 7 suitcases, over the other side of the world, and 1 week left in our holiday house we rented, with only $5000 left in the back, no job, no house to rent, nothing. This was a bit of predicament to be in.

BY N.D.H

My daily prayer routine became more and more sincere every day. We needed a break and we needed it now. I knew we had been guided here by the feeling, and we were about to run out of money, and had nowhere to live. But I knew that the feeling had never let me down before. So we kept on, and my search for a job began to bear a little fruit. I had 2 companies interested in taking me on, but none of them were making the decision.

We had only a few days left, in this holiday house on the island. One morning during my daily routine of prayer, it came. The feeling came, it felt as it did before, warmth from my head down my neck and shoulders into my chest and arms, it felt like the morning sunrise did on my skin, but on the inside of body.

I knew that we were being watched by the Universal Energy all along. A feeling of calmness and peace came, I knew everything would be ok.

That day, I had a call from one of the potential employers. They said, "we can give you a job but it's in Rockhampton, in Central Queensland". It was about a 10-hour drive from where we were on this island. I immediately said, "yes I will take it".

CHAPTER 12

My wife researched the area for the best place to live, what schools were available for the children, and for a house to rent.

She had found a 5-bedroom house on an acreage in Yeppoon. Which is on the coast just 30mins drive from Rockhampton. So we called and the estate agent sent forms to fill in. We needed to pay a deposit of around $2000 to secure the place, and we signed a year's contract to stay there.

The last day of our time to stay in the house arrived. We packed up the 7 suitcases and jumped on the ferry, this time it wasn't the school rush. We had a car that my brother had bought for us a few weeks before we came to Australia, an old Kluger 4wd auto. Although it was a 7-seater, there was no room for all of us and the suitcases. So we packed up the suitcases and my oldest and I were to travel up to Yeppoon, unload and come back to pick up the rest of the family. The family stayed with my brother for the night, and my oldest son and I started the long 10-hour drive to Yeppoon.

It was so exiting! We left at 5.30pm and it was like we were going on an adventure. We had so much fun driving up there. My boy made videos, and we played and sang music for the first 4 hours. We started to get a little tired, but had another 6 hours to go. It was dark and the roads were strange. Big trucks came up behind us with full beam on, and would overtake when they could, roaring past us. We pulled over to fill up the car with petrol at Childers, about halfway. There was a group of men sitting outside the service station all sitting around a table, with short shorts, singlets and thongs (flip flops). The singlets were dirty, and they were drinking beer. It turned out that they were ok, they were polite, but it was one of those moments where you think "ok, this could go either way", but it went the way of goodness, thank goodness. My oldest and I went to the toilet, it was outside. The lights of the toilet attracted all sorts of strange bugs. We ducked and dived our way there, peed really fast, and ran back to the car. Laughing and joking. Ok hallway there, and we were already tired.

We finally came to Rockhampton, we pulled off the motorway and saw the big Welcome to Rockhampton Bull on the roundabout. We thought we would be there any minute, but another 30 mins was on the sat nav. We were both so tired, we were overtired. It was dark and no cars were on the road. It was about 2am in the morning, we had been driving in the dark for so long. Finally the sat nav guided us to Yeppoon, and the house that we had rented for the first year. We drove up the drive to the house, and our eyes were wide, trying to take in the place we were going to live. We tried to sleep in the car, on the drive of the house, as we couldn't pick up the keys until 9am in the morning. We tried to sleep as best we could with legs over each other, pillows against the door, but every position was uncomfortable. The car was hot and filled with humidity. We didn't want to turn the car on, not to wake up our new neighbours. We didn't want to open the windows because of all the strange bugs. So it was a very unconfutable few hours.

The sunrise was a welcome sight. And we opened the windows, it was still warm. Central QLD in the summer is a hot and humid place to be. When we open the windows, we could hear a whistling. It sounded like there was a man, whistling around the back of the house. So we got out to explore where this whistling was coming from. We walked around the house looking into the windows, to see the living space, it was a beautiful house, on a beautiful acreage, but the whistling man was alluding us. The whistle kept coming and we carried on looking around the house to see where it was coming from. After 2 or 3 laps around the house, we finally saw the culprit. It was a magpie! A magpie could whistle such a beautiful little song, that sounded just like a man whistling. Wow, this country was amazing me more and more every day. There were palm trees in the garden, tropical plants along the side of the house showing off wonderful colours. I was in heaven for sure.

We went into town to collect the keys from the estate agents, and went back to the house. We opened the door and went in, it was massive! The house was huge, all tiled floors, brand new stone kitchen, new carpets, it was amazing my boy and I were filled with smiles, but still red eyed and shaking from tiredness. The house had no furniture, it was completely empty, and we had no furniture either. So we drove back into Rockhampton. We went to fantastic furniture and bought 5 mattresses. The thin foam ones, so we could fit them in the car. I figured as long as we had something to sleep on, it would be ok. So we took them back to the house and laid them on the floor. We both dived onto them and fell asleep, we were both utterly exhausted.

We woke up some hours later, and the thought of driving all the way back down to Brisbane, to pick up the rest of the family, and then to drive back to Yeppoon was painful. I called my wife and asked her to check how much the flights were. They weren't that expensive, so I asked if she would fly with the children and we would collect them at the airport. She found good flights and flew up the next morning. We picked up the remaining family and drove back to the house. The empty 5-bedroom house with just 5 mattresses on the floor. At least we had something soft to sleep on. My wife was very supportive, we had a job, a house, and five mattresses.

We had very little money, but we had each other.

We loved each other, the children were all so good, having fun exploring the house and grounds. We explored the town and the beaches. We made some friends, but money was very tight. We needed to pay rent every week, and we worked it out, that we had just enough to pay rent for one more month. But Christmas was right on us. Christmas was just a short few weeks away and we had nothing for the children. The children had always had amazing Christmases, with a living room full of presents to come down to every year on Christmas morning. But this year we had nothing, and it was just a short few weeks away and we had very little money to buy anything. We did our best, my wife was very good at making the most of what we had, and she went right to work buying as much as she could with the little money we had. A family from the estate agents came to visit us at the house, and saw that we had nothing. A little embarrassed, we offered them a drink and tried to make them welcome. They must of felt the Christmas spirit, because that family went about immediately trying to help us. They called their friends, and their friends started to knock our door and say, "here we have a microwave you can have", and another came and said "hey, we have a fridge you can have". This family came around with boxes of plates and dishes, and boxes of presents for the children. I am a very proud man, and I do not like being on the receiving end of charity. But this time, my heart was softened and filled with gratitude. We had a great Christmas, and the children didn't complain about a thing. In fact they loved it.

Christmas came a went, and it was time to start work. I was so nervous, I was shown the around the office and the warehouse where the machinery was stored. I was introduced to the men, and they made me feel right at home. The engineer that I was to replace showed me the work that I was expected to do, and all I can remember is saying "are you serious?" I said, "I have never done this before", excel worksheets working out calculations for heat stress on steel, and more. My heart rose up to my throat as I thought "oh my goodness, what am I going to do ". Then I was introduced to him. I will say him as to keep his identity private, but "him" was my new boss. A tall man, with glasses, I could see him looking at me trying to figure me out, he couldn't understand my accent, and I laugh now, because we became great friends and he still struggles to understand me.

My boss really did take me under his wing, he was well known and respected in the rail industry in central QLD, and he must of seen something in me as he helped me become something I never knew I could be. He had compassion and patience, a lot of patience as he taught me everything he could. It was either that, or the fact that I was all he could get, because not everyone wants to live and work in Rockhampton. So he took me in and began to teach me all he could. He taught me invaluable lessons. I know how to work hard and get jobs done no matter what it takes, that is my skill. I will get a job done, I will own it and complete it as best as I could, and I would never give up until it was done. A lesson my father taught me growing up. "Hard Work Wins, Where Wishy Washy Wishing Wont." I understood principles of engineering from my construction days and from building the house, but calculations as you know, I need a maths tutor to help me.

Work went well, and I fit right in after completing the first project. I gained the confidence of my boss and my workforce, from then on it went very well.

My pay checks kept coming in, and we started to buy furniture, for the house. What a day it was when we bought a sofa ! My wife and I still slept on a mattress, but slowly and surely we were staring to rebuild.

On the drive into the town we would always pass a masonic lodge. It would always catch my eye, I learnt a little about free masonry through the teachings of the religion I was brought up in. It is well known that some of the founding leaders of the religion were in fact free masons. So every time I drove past there, it drew my attention.

One day I decided to look up the secretary of the lodge. I called him to express my interest, he told me he could come around and talk with me about it. So he did, he brought with him a friend and I asked questions and they were very friendly and kind. I was impressed, and I had a good feeling about them. I felt that I needed a fraternity of men around me that I could trust, and indeed I felt that I could trust these men.

After a few visits I decided to ask if I could join, and a date was given for me to join. The secretary asked me if I knew a certain induvial, and I said "yes ! I know him, he is my boss." He said that he was a member. I went into work the next day and told my boss that I was joining, and he was glad. He smiled and said that he would attend the day I would join.

The day I was to join came, and I was nervous, although I was prepared, I didn't really know what it would be like.

I went, and was looked after very well. Many people already know what masonry is about and people draw their own conclusions. But for me, Masonry is all about taking good men, and making them better. The knowledge gained within masonry should not be talked about outside of the lodge. It is only to honour it, as the knowledge gained, if used correctly will only serve to make the man a better man.

As I said, I was nervous, and the time came for me to join. I wanted to know if I was doing the right thing. As I was learning, during my joining, it came. Yes, the feeling came, the same feeling as had always come to me. It wasn't overwhelming, it was indeed the same feeling that has guided me through my life, and I knew, I knew I was doing the right thing.

So I joined and grew in understanding of free masonry. To all those sceptics, I just want to say, its good. If the principles of masonry are respected and followed correctly it is good. And if its good it can't be bad. I enjoyed attending and learning, it reminded me of the religion I had been brought up in, and I felt good about it.

A Fine explanation of the principles of Free Masonry are explain below by Bro J.F Smith

ASHLARS - ROUGH, SMOOTH - STORY OF A STONE

By Bro J. Fairbairn Smith

An eminent sculptor was once asked: "How do you carve such beautiful statues?" He replies, "It is the simplest thing in the world. I take a hammer and chisel and from a massive, shapeless rock, I knock off all the stone I do not want, and there is the statue. It was there all the time."

In every Masonic Lodge room there is, or should be, the Rough Ashlar and the Perfect Ashlar. What is their significance? What do they have to do with Masonry?

In our ritual work we are taught that the Rough Ashlar

BY N.D.H

"is a stone as taken from the quarry in its rude and natural state" *The Rough Ashlar was not a stone that was merely picked up somewhere. It was a stone that has been selected. Some work was done upon it. It was apparently a good stone. It was a stone that showed good prospects of being capable of being made into a Perfect Ashlar. If it had not been a good stone, it would never have been cut out from the quarry.*

So it is with our prospective member. He cannot be merely picked up somewhere. He must be selected. Before he is ready to be initiated some work must be done upon him. He must stand certain basic tests. He must be apparently of good material. He must be a man who shows good prospects of being capable of being made into a good Mason. If he had not been a good man, he should never have been proposed for membership.

In changing a Rough Ashlar into a Perfect Ashlar, the workman takes away and never adds to. He chips and chips. He cuts away the rough edges. He removes the visible flaws, he does not create by chemical means or otherwise, a new material. He takes that which is already there and develops it into the Perfect Ashlar.

The stone from which the Venus de Milo was carved by an unknown sculptor of ancient times, lay since the beginning of time in the rocks of the Island Milo. A common, unknown workman may have cut a huge piece of marble from the quarry. But it took a master artisan to carve out the beautiful statue. It took a good piece of marble and a skilled artist to produce the marvellous statue.

MORE THAN JUST A FEELING

Not many operators in Masonry can make a Perfect Ashlar. So there are not many perfect Masons in our Lodges. In our ritual and other work, we can take away much of the roughness, remove the sharp points and obliterate the visible defects. We can produce as good a Mason as there is within our power to produce. But the essential thing is to have a good material upon which to work.

This statement is applicable to all mankind, but to us as Symbolic Masons, it is pregnant with meaning, for, was not each one, at the commencement of his Masonic career, placed in the Northeast corner as an example stone, in the hope that the stone so placed would, in the fullness of time, be wrought into a thing of beauty acceptable to the builder?

What does the poet say of the stone? Isn't it strange that Princes and Kings and clowns that caper in sawdust rings, and common folks like you and me Are builders for eternity? Each is given a kit of tools, A shapeless mass and a book of rules: And each must make, ere life is flown; A stumbling block or a steppingstone.

These are very true words. The kit of tools are those talents with which God has blessed us to enable us to fulfil our mission in life. We are told in the Volume of the Sacred Law that one man received five talents, another, two talents, and yet another, only one talent, so that our duty is for each to discharge his allotted task to the best of his ability, and help those who have not been so well blessed as himself.

BY N.D.H

Thus each will be assisted in carving out the "Grand Design" of being happy and communicating happiness and thereby of being more "extensively serviceable to his fellow creatures."

The shapeless mass is a man's character, and each one of us is his own Architect, Builder and Material, and like our predecessors, the Operative Masons, we each must show our craftsmanship in working out a perfect "Ashlar" fit to be tried by the square of his own conscience.

The book of rules is the V.S.L. "That great light that will guide us to all truth, direct our steps in the path of happiness, and thus, point out the whole duty of man."

Let us pause for a moment and earnestly ask ourselves, which are we making--stumbling block or a steppingstone? If a man's life is such that he cannot "join in the grand design of being happy and communicating happiness to others," then he is a stumbling block, not only to himself, but to all those with whom he is associated. If that man is a Freemason he should study the ritual and discover the inner meaning, so that he can learn to perfect his stone.

Let us trace whence comes this perfect stone. An ancient charge provides that a mould stone shall be given to a visiting Operative Mason to enable him to demonstrate his craftsmanship. The stones were selected individual stones from the quarries to suit the requirement of the material building. As Speculative Masons, we obtain our mould stones from the quarries of life. Thus, when we receive an application for admission to our Lodge it is our duty to carefully scrutinize all the credentials of the applicant from every angle, so that only approved material is admitted to the Craft.

Freemasonry can and does improve good material, but it cannot make bad material good. As with the Operative Mason, poor material would have endangered the material structure. So with us as Speculative Masons, a faulty Ashlar will endanger the Spiritual temple we are endeavouring to build.

Having found, by the strictest inquiry, that the applicant, or mould stone, is suitable, we have, by those inquiries, knocked off some of the irregularities which surrounded him, and after his initiation, he is represented as the "rough Ashlar," that is, the stone is no longer the mould stone, but it is approximately a cube which still requires a considerable amount of "dressing" before the "perfect Ashlar" which is within it can be brought to light, and the candidate is given him to "knock off rough knobs and evanescence," of his character.

Later on he finds that, although the common gavel and chisel are suitable for reducing the roughness they are not capable of achieving perfection. As a Craftsman he receives another set of working tools, one of which is essential to perfection, namely, the square, and here he learns that it is only by continual grinding and many applications of the square that the stone can be brought to a true die, or cube.

In his capacity as a Craftsman and as a man of the

world, he is continually coming into contact with his fellows and he learns to control his passions and to recognize the rights of others, with the result that the stone he is working upon, namely, his character, is gradually taking shape as a perfect Ashlar.

Later, he is called upon to hand his stone over to the Builder, who cuts a bevelled hole at the top, so that the stone can be attached to a Lewis and be hoisted up ready to be placed on the base assigned to it by the Builder. Thus, he is reminded that the rope, the Lewis, and the crane represent the all sustaining power of God, and that if he has discharged his duty faithfully and in accordance with the precepts laid down in the V.S.L., he may rest assured that when his final summons comes he will find that the great Builder will have prepared a place for him in that "Great Spiritual Temple not made with hands eternal in the Heavens."

Life was going very well. Work was going well, we started to furnish the house, and started to save money for a deposit to build a new home.

We started to look for land, and I started to design the home on paper like I did the first build, but this time it was going to be spectacular. Concrete, glass, high high ceilings with views of the sunrise and sunset. Swimming pool, lush gardens and a place to call home for all the family.

The time came very close, to actually deciding on a piece of land. We looked at 5 acre plots, 22 acre plots in the mountain, 1 acre plots with unobstructed 180 degree sea views. We just needed to decide on what we wanted. The money was in the bank, our house was fully furnished, except that my wife and I still slept on a mattress, but we had 2 living rooms, a media room, the children's bedrooms were all done nicely, I even had a ride on lawn mower! What fun the kids had riding that mower, if you want the kids to cut the lawn, get a ride on.

CHAPTER 13

My wife's mother fell ill with cancer, and she started to become very unwell. So my wife decided to go back to the UK for 2 weeks to visit her mother and family for what may be the last time she would see her mother. My brother came up to help look after the children while I worked. We had a great time, the kids loved their uncle, he was so much fun.

I was at the time preparing to tender for the largest rail project that the company had ever tendered for. The small company I worked for, a 1-million-dollar project was massive, and the expected profit margin I had to make was 35%.

I worked on it, planned it, and submitted the tender. A call came through to let me know that we had won it! Wow! I called my boss and was so excited! I really felt that life was really working for me. I was promoted and had a large pay increase. We had a deposit for a self-build for the house of our dreams. We had furniture and had great days out with the children. Life was on the up and up, and I was determined to achieve.

My wife flew to the UK, and all I could see on her

social media posts were of her catching up with her friends out in pubs and restaurants. I thought she was to spend every Minuit she had with her dying mother. I said nothing but I knew she was loving the attention she used to have when she was there. All the farmers and young lads from the village were all over her, and I knew my wife loved that sort of attention.

She was gone for 2 weeks, and when she was to arrive back I would be gone for 2 weeks to complete this 1-million-dollar contract.

It was time to pick my wife up from the airport, all the kids were excited, and we waited at the gate for her to come through.

When she came through, the kids ran to her and she cuddled them. After they all had their cuddle, I put my arm around her to usher her out of the way of people who wanted to come through, to which she pushed my arm away and said, "get off". "Get Off", was the first thing she said to me. I instantly knew something was wrong.

That night she told me that she wanted to go back to the UK to live. I tried to tell her that our lives are here now, and this is the best place for the kids to grow up with all the wonderful opportunities this country would offer. She was determined, and sulked for the whole weekend. "I want to go home" is all she would say. I said, "it's taken us 5 years of bloody hard work and determination to get us here, all the sacrifices we have made to get here, all we have gone through and we are about to build a dream home for us here."

Nothing I said would persuade her, "I want to go home is all she would say."

I needed to leave to go and work on this million-dollar project, and would be away for 2 weeks.

All the time I worked on this immensely important project, all I could think of was, "what am I going to do? I can't believe she is playing up like this again, maybe she has met someone over there? Maybe all she wants is the attention from all the farmers lads again, she felt popular over there being the only tall blonde, and over here in Australia she wasn't getting any attention like that because all the girls were tall, and had long blonde hair. How I am going to get her to stay?"

Whilst working on this project, we stayed in an old Queenslander hospital. It reminded me of a world war 2 hospital, I really liked it there.

One night after speaking with my wife on the phone, I laid there in bed and wondered what I was to do.

As I was laying there looking up at the ceiling, the feeling came. Just like all the other times, it came, and I felt it, and I recognised it as the feeling that has guided me throughout my life. The very feeling that had guided me to Australia. I felt softened, and I felt calm and peaceful. During this state of peace, I felt the words, "if she wants to go, let her go."

When I felt those words, I knew I had to tell her that if she wanted to go, she could go, but I was staying. My choice was to stay, and I had to accept her choice to go if that's what she wanted to do.

The project finished and was a complete success, it was fantastic. We completed the project 8 hours in front of schedule. The teams worked so hard, we had a party and I bought lots of rum and beers for the team.

On my return home to the family, my wife again told me she wanted to go home. So I said "ok, if that what you want to do, you can go home, but I will be staying."

She didn't seem fazed by me saying I would be staying, but lit up and smiled, and said "ok I'm going home."

I asked her to really think about her choice, as it would break the family up, I told her that we would divorce as this would mean the end of the marriage. It took her only a few days to let me know that she was ok with the divorce and that she was going. She was going, and she was taking the children with her. When she said that she was taking the children with her, my face went numb, and the air seemed cold. The thought of my children leaving was too hard to even imagine, but I knew, that I had to let her do whatever she wanted to do.

I agreed, and remembered the feeling that came to me and told me that I should let her go.

Before I could even sit down and talk to the children, she had already told them they were going home, and that they would see their old school friends and cousins and family. Of course they were all so excited, they didn't really comprehend what this really meant. All they could imagine was seeing their friends and family again after 18 months, so of course were excited. I was disappointed that she had prepared them before I could even sit with them and speak with them about it. They knew that they were going, and I was staying. But the excitement of the whole idea must of clouded the thought of us being on the opposite sides of the world, and that we wouldn't see each other for a very long time.

We talked one night my wife and I, and we started to plan for her move back to the UK with the kids. She needed flights, a house to move into, a car, furniture for the children, money in the bank to survive on and had already worked everything out. She wanted a certain amount of money every month from me for support and had everything planned.

I agreed with whatever she wanted to do. So she booked the tickets. I will never forget the day she told me she had booked them. She smiled and seemed so happy, she had booked the tickets for the 6th Feb.

I went for regular walks on the beach by myself to try and comprehend what was going on. but all I could think about was why did I have the feeling to let her go. This feeling had never led me astray before, in fact it had only brought goodness, guidance and miracles to my life.

But here I was, listening to the feeling that had told me to let her go. This would mean that I would be letting my family go! My beautiful wonderful children, I would be letting them go to. I would be losing everything I had known for the last 16 years. But the feeling told me to let her go. So I walked the beach most nights, wondering and praying about what is going on here?

This one evening I walked a beach called Roslyn Bay. My favourite beach up there in Yeppoon, and I prayed. I prayed and asked "what is going on here? I'm about to lose my everything, and we were just about to get to where we wanted to be, money in the ban a wonderful home great job, all this came to us in 18months, from 7 suitcase and no money to being in a great position, about to build our dream home, and the feeling told me to let her go. "

During my walk on Roslyn bay, whilst I was pondering and praying about this. The feeling came to me, it was just like a little brush of the usual feeling that I had experienced the many times before. It felt like it just gently brushed over me, and I just felt that everything was going to be ok. I gained confidence in the feeling, as I knew it had never let me down before. So I went back to the house, thinking that whatever happens, and it's going to be ok.

My wife was always in charge of the bank account. She had online access, and she started to filter money over to her UK account little by little from our main account. I knew she was doing it, but I didn't say anything. Then she started selling the furniture off. People were coming collecting items from the house and giving her cash, again I didn't say anything. She kept telling me, "I want to go my own way and do my own thing" to which I agreed, because I knew I had to let her go.

Slowly but surely, every time I came home from work, the house would look a little emptier as she continued to sell everything online and collect the cash.

She told me she had found a house in the UK, and a car, so she took money from the savings and sent it across to her UK Account. The bank account and the house were emptying slowly but surely just like the sand out of an hourglass. Everything we had worked so hard for, was disappearing before me day by day.

A week before they were about to leave, the house was almost empty. She had packed up personal belongings and sent them over via post, and the furniture had almost all disappeared. The money we saved for a deposit for our new house had diminished to $2000.

All that was left in the house was the fridge, a washing machine, and the mattress we had slept on for the last 2 years. This massive 5-bedroom house was empty, it echoed when we talked. There was nothing there, except the fridge, washing machine and the mattress on the bedroom floor.

The hourglass was hanging on desperately to the very last few grains of sand. My material life had emptied again, once again I had no material items. and no money in the bank. But I still had the presence of the children in my life, and I was ok with that, as long as I saw their wonderful smiles, life seemed full.

The morning of the dreaded day of their departure came. I packed the car with their suitcases, and took them to the airport, I left them with my oldest son at the airport, he looked after them whilst I went back to collect the rest of the family. The airport was only a 30 min drive from our house, so I can't even imagine what was going through his mind while he sat there looking after the suitcases for 1 whole hour on his own. From a young child I have always been impressed with his strength of character and his ability to get up and carry on.

I arrived back at the house to be greeted by the excited children. They were excited to go back to see family and friends, not really understanding the reality of the situation.

They all got in the car, my wife sat in the front, I wore sunglasses so that my children would see if was crying. A song by Sam Smith came on the radio, it was the goodbye song, I quickly turned it off, and tried to keep spirits high.

We arrived at the airport and we all went in to meet my oldest son. We had a few moments to say goodbye. I remember I knelt down to my daughter's eye level and told her "Always remember this my love, Daddy loves you and misses you".

After a few photos of me with the children, it came time to go through security. I helped get the bags through and had my final cuddles with the children. My wife hugged me and told me that she was sorry it had come to this, and they all went through the small security screening. Rockhampton airport is small, and there was a large glass wall that separated the departure lounge from the main airport lounge so I could see them. My youngest son came to the window, and put his hand on the glass. I put my hand on his from the other side of the glass, and started to cry behind my sunglasses. He noticed that I was crying and then he started to cry. I tried to keep my emotions in check so that they could be strong and not worry or be upset. I could see them walking down the walkway to the plane, they all waved goodbye and I took some photos, whilst waving. They boarded the plane.

I quickly ran to the car and drove around to an area where you can watch the planes take off. I got out of the car and waved to the plane, not knowing if they could see me. But I waved and waved. The plane gained speed down the runway, and lifted form the ground. I waved and waved , and watched the plane fly into the sky. Tears flowed down my checks as I watched the plane take off.

As the plane went higher and higher, I started to frantically walk back and forth around the car. My babies were on that plane and they were going they were going. I didn't take my eyes off that plane until it finally vanished into the blue blue skies. At the disappearance of the plane into the blue blue skies, I could no longer control the emotions that were flooding my body. I was frantic, I felt like my children were drowning and there was nothing I could do. The feelings overtook me, and I screamed and shouted, walking back and forth, my children ! my babies is all I could say, in a frantic state. Tears were uncontrollably falling from my eyes. I was so desperate to get on the next plane and go catch them up. I thought about driving to Brisbane to see them at the airport for their connecting flight, but knew I had to let them go.

The 30 min drive back to the house, seemed like 30 hours. I was hysterical. I screamed and cried like a baby. I couldn't control what was taking over my body. I had just lost my babies, they had gone, and I knew I wouldn't see them for a very long time. I tried so many times to calm myself down and said to myself, "come on Lovely Boy be strong" but then the tears and whaling would overtake me again. I had no control over it, I cried and screamed and whaled for the whole drive back to the house.

I pulled up on the drive and walked into the house crying my heart and soul out. It felt like a sword had been driven through my chest, but multiplied by 5. The pain was unbearable.

I open the door to the house and found the emptiness hollowing. My screams echoed throughout the empty house, and walked to the mattress a threw myself down clutching my chest. The emotional pain felt so physical. The pain in my chest was like something I had never felt before.

There I stayed for hours crying and screaming into the pillows.

I felt a numbness come over me as the hours passed. Tears started to dry up, but the occasional sob would reappear out of nowhere. I tracked their flights on the flight tracker app for the following 24 hours and remember watching the plane on the app as it landed in Manchester. They were there, my babies, my babies, my babies, all the way over the other side of the world.

I tried to call my family for a bit of support, but they were in bed due to the time zone difference. I tried to call my brothers here in Australia, but there was no answer, they must have been busy. I was totally alone in my pain and anguish. I couldn't call anyone or speak to anyone. I was totally alone sitting on this mattress, crying. Never have I ever felt so alone in all my life. At the worst possible moment of my life, I was all alone. I felt totally and utterly abandoned. The feeling that has always guided me from harm, inspired me to take action, the feeling that led to miracles throughout my life, had led me to this abandoned state. And to make it worse, the feeling didn't come to save me, to let me know that I would be ok. all I felt was total abandonment.

Dusk fell, and I didn't turn on any lights. Darkness filled the house, as I sat there crying, trying to console myself. As I sat there in the little light that remained from the setting sun, I knelt, and I prayed. As I prayed, I felt the presence of men. The presence was so strong, that I could almost see them with my natural eyes. They were ancient men, dressed in armour, they had swords that they held with the point held down to the ground with their hands resting on the top of the handles. I was surrounded by them, they formed a circle around me. I felt that they were my ancient brothers, coming to console me. There was a very sombre feeling in the room, a feeling of ancient honour. It was very strong, and I knew it wasn't in my imagination.

In my total abandonment, in my darkest moment, I surely was not alone. I felt no love, I felt no security, I felt no feelings of comfort, I felt no feelings of assurance. Instead I felt pain of which I have never felt before. Emotional pain that was so strong it passed into my physical body. And in this moment, there was nobody to hold my hand, nobody to speak comfort to me, instead I felt surrounded. Circled around by my ancient masonic brothers. They had their heads bowed, as if they knew how I was feeling, but could not bring comfort. It was if they knew I had to pass through this moment all on my own. It was as if they had felt the same as I did once, and knew my pain, but could not bring comfort, but just honour the pain.

Although the feeling didn't come to rescue me, words came to me, powerful words that passed like subtitles before my eyes. It said/read "the joy that you will feel, will be greater than, or equal to the pain that you are feeling right now".

Khalil Gibran wrote a poem about pain. And this is how it goes.

Your pain is the breaking of the shell that encloses your understanding.

Even as the stone of the fruit must break, that its heart may stand in the sun, so must you know pain.

And could you keep your heart in wonder at the daily miracles of your life, your pain would not seem less wondrous than your joy;

And you would accept the seasons of your heart, even as you have always accepted the seasons that pass over your fields.

And you would watch with serenity through the winters of your grief.

Much of your pain is self-chosen.

It is the bitter potion by which the physician within you heals your sick self.

Therefore trust the physician, and drink his remedy in silence and tranquility:

For his hand, though heavy and hard, is guided by the tender hand of the Unseen,

And the cup he brings, though it burn your lips, has been fashioned of the clay which the Potter has moistened with His own sacred tears.

He also wrote about Joy from Pain... Khalid Gilbran.

Then a woman said, "Speak to us of Joy and Sorrow."

Even as the stone of the fruit must break, that its heart may stand in the sun, so must you know pain.

And could you keep your heart in wonder at the daily miracles of your life, your pain would not seem
less wondrous than your joy;

And you would accept the seasons of your heart, even as you have always accepted the seasons that pass over your fields.

BY N.D.H

And you would watch with serenity through the winters of your grief.

Much of your pain is self-chosen.

*It is the bitter potion by which the physician within
you heals your sick self.*

*Therefore trust the physician, and drink his remedy
in silence and tranquility:*

For his hand, though heavy and hard, is guided by the tender hand of the Unseen,

*And the cup he brings, though it burn your lips, has
been fashioned of the clay which the Potter has moistened with His own sacred tears.*

*He also wrote about Joy from Pain... Khalid Gilbran.
Then a woman said, "Speak to us of Joy and Sorrow."*

And he answered:

Your joy is your sorrow unmasked.

And the selfsame well from which your laughter rises was oftentimes filled with your tears.

And how else can it be?

The deeper that sorrow carves into your being, the more joy you can contain.

Is not the cup that hold your wine the very cup that was burned in the potter's oven?

And is not the lute that soothes your spirit, the very wood that was hollowed with knives?

When you are joyous, look deep into your heart and you shall find it is only that which has given you sorrow that is giving you joy.

When you are sorrowful look again in your heart, and you shall see that in truth you are weeping for that which has been your delight.

Some of you say, "Joy is greater than sorrow," and others say, "Nay, sorrow is the greater."

But I say unto you, they are inseparable.

Together they come, and when one sits alone with

you at your board, remember that the other is asleep upon your bed.

Verily you are suspended like scales between your sorrow and your joy.

Only when you are empty are you at standstill and balanced.

When the treasure-keeper lifts you to weigh his gold and his silver, needs must your joy or your sorrow rise or fall.

CHAPTER 14

Thine own hearts sorrows mention but in prayer, then spread sunshine with thee everywhere. That's what my Dad always said, and I listened. I had a job, I had to make sure I kept that job, so I switched the switch when I walked in the office, and then it automatically switched back off when I left. Coming home to an empty house after 16 years of being greeted by wonderful happy children was pure misery. The house was empty, as was I.

I took to drinking, drinking was the only thing that numbed the pain for a short few hours. This became a daily routine, happy man at work, and a lonely drunk at night.

As all this was going on, my younger brother had a lot going on also. His then wife had left him. He had lost his first marriage with his childhood sweetheart, then took courage to marry again, and this one left. Now let me tell you a few things about my little brother. Never ever has there been anyone like him. He is a genius, I have seen his mind work and when he thinks of something he will do it.

He has always been a barber, from the age of 14 he

worked for my father. As I told you before, he knew everyone, all the gangsters in the town loved him.

After his 2nd suicide attempt, he married an Australian woman, they travelled and then moved to Australia. He continued to work as a barber, until he decided that he wanted to something different. He studied and studied, and within a few short months he qualified as a financial advisor. Within 1 year he was one of the highest earning financial advisors in Australia. This man knows the power of the secret.

However after his wife left, his life quickly took a turn for the worse. He felt that there is no use in living anymore, and fought every day to battle against the feeling of suicide. He met a wonderful lady, who he is now marrying, and she came into his life just at the right time. Talk about divine timing, they fell in love within the first few dates, and my brother seemed happy.

We would talk every day, and he would explain to me how he was feeling. I would try and cheer him up and keep him positive. Until one day, his girlfriend called me at my work and said he has just tried to kill himself. He had a breakdown, and took a knife to his throat. I ran out of work, and jumped into the truck, and drove 8 hours to Brisbane without stopping. I called my Dad and told him he might have to come over. I got to Brisbane and ran into my brother's house, and he was sitting there happy as Larry ! I said, "what the bloody hell is going on", his girlfriend told me about his break down, and how his ex-wife was there pestering him. He grabbed the knife and put it to his throat. His wife screamed, and did nothing, but then his new girlfriend ran at him, tackled him to the floor and quickly disarmed him. Then I knew for sure that she was the one for him!

I took my brother and his girlfriend back up to Yeppoon with me so I could keep an eye on him. He didn't stop talking all the way up, it was if he was on cocaine or speed or something. I gave him 2 diazepam, but they didn't do anything, he was talking and laughing and joking all the way up. Even when we got there he didn't stop. I gave him more diazepam but still they didn't work. I talked to his girlfriend and said "we need to call an ambulance" so we did. The ambulance came, and the paramedics knew exactly what was going on. They knew he was suffering from a mental illness. I told them he had tried to kill himself a few days earlier, and they were absolutely fantastic. They talked him into going to hospital. We followed the ambulance and went into the emergency room, where he was assessed by the psychiatric team. He was laughing and making jokes, he was hysterical, and sometimes I couldn't help but laugh. But this was serious, I explained to the doctor what had happened, and how he was nonstop talking even after 4 diazepam. The doctor said that he should be knocked out cold, but he was flying. The doctor told me that this was serious, a medical emergency, and I did the right thing by calling an ambulance.

They wanted me to sign the papers for him to be sectioned in the mental health department. When my brother figured out he was about to be sectioned, he hit the roof. He put himself in the corner and told the doctor that he would eat him, and everyone there if he sectioned him. I said "brother, that isn't helping your case".

So finally after 6 hours of persuasion, he agreed to be sectioned. I walked with him down to the ward and I remember as I left, he looked at me and said, "I'll get you back for this". He hasn't yet, and I hope he doesn't, because he is a genius remember. His girlfriend was distraught, she couldn't speak much English, and hear she was in a strange land, with a new boyfriend who she loved, who now was sectioned into a mental health ward. She went to visit him every single day, taking him food and fresh clothes, and sneaking him in cigarettes, yep this girl loved my brother alright.

On day I went to visit him, and they had a guitar there, my brother is an awesome guitarist, and plays rock and roll blues like nothing you have every heard before. I walked into the ward to hear him singing and playing the guitar. All the mental patients in the ward were dancing around, my brother had all the mental patients dancing around the ward to his rock and roll blues. What a man my brother is, crazy, but what a man. The nurse said that it was the best day they had ever had in there.

He was finally diagnosed with severe rapid bipolar, and then it all made sense. I could see his life like a timeline of ups and downs. The recent events of his life tipped him over the edge. He took tablets and tablets and tablets, if you shook him he would rattle for sure.

Anyway they discharged him, and they drove home back to Brisbane. I thought he would be ok, but he was committed right back into hospital the day after he got back. His girlfriend stuck with him and continues to be with him, making sure he is ok. Now that my friends is true love, and I attend their wedding next week.

CHAPTER 15

Where was I ? oh yes, I was still in Yeppoon, and I had moved into a small furnished apartment near the beach front. It was close to the pubs, and I always made a regular appearance there. Getting blind drunk, and playing up. I did go to the gym every day. Drinking became a habit, as did smoking, but this time no drugs. I stayed away from the drugs this time, and I'm glad I did. Otherwise I may have not made it back.

I tried to get used to the loneliness, and would Face-Time the children as much as I could. It was great to speak with them, I would speak to my wife about how she was doing, we tried to be friends and tried to be there for each other during this difficult time. I would send the agreed amount of money over to help her and the children.

Drinking seemed to dull the pain of the loss I had felt, this medicine was my daily dosage. It worked, for at least a little while.

I decided that I needed to move to Brisbane to be nearer my brothers, and a job came up. A massive opportunity to work on a great infrastructure project. I was interviewed and given the job. It was the best paid job I had ever had, the money was fantastic. I packed up the car with all I had and drove to Brisbane, I moved into my brothers and slept on the sofa while I tried to get back on my feet.

Drinking was second nature to me by this time, and I drank every single night.

Although life was fun, and to some would seem like a dream life. Deep inside I was tormented. The nights were the worst, after drinking I would make my bed on the sofa and lay there, thinking of my children. Tears would come, and I would cry myself to sleep.

One night, I got very drunk, and everyone went to bed, it was dark, and the emotions came up very strong. I began to hate myself, why, why, why would I let my children go. I must be a really bad person, and this time, was the first time in my life that I hit myself. I punched and punched and punched myself in the face, and cried and cried. I woke up in the morning with a massive black eyes, and thought how the hell am I going to explain this in work.

What was I doing, why was I behaving like this, why did I mask myself? Let me tell you, I mask myself very well. Everyone thought I was happy because I would laugh and joke and tell funny stories. It was great, but again I knew, "Thine own hearts sorrow mention but in prayer, then spread sunshine with thee everywhere", and that was exactly what I was doing, and doing a bloody good job at it.

My brothers girlfriend had enough of my antics and bringing girls back to her house, the last straw was when she woke up one morning and one the girls I brought home walked naked to the bathroom Infront of my brother. That was it ! I had to find my own place. I don't blame her one bit, I was out of control. So I did, I found an awesome apartment in the city, I had no furniture. I bought a fridge, a washing machine and a queen size bed, that's all I had. And that was all I needed.

I thought that I was going to get my life back on track, and I thought I was doing a good job Until I told my wife that payments would be reduced now due to her getting back on her feet and having a new man moving in with her, so I did. I reduced payments.

She was furious, and she blocked me from all the children's phones, she cut all contact with my children. As if it wasn't bad enough that I didn't see them, and my only joy was speaking with them on FaceTime, she stopped all that and I couldn't even message them. This just made things worse, I would get drunk and cry every night.

It had been almost 9 months since they left, and I hadn't processed the pain properly I had just been covering it with alcohol and innuendos.

I longed for company, I was so lonely.

The job took me onto 10 days on, and 4 days off roster. I lived with a good friend, he was great company, he was very kind, and saw my pain, and tried to help me as much as he could. Giving sound advice being kind and caring, we had a great time on our 10 days on. The 4 days off, were not so exciting, drinking in the city playing up, and being lonely in my apartment. I would sit on the floor and drink beer, and cry. I was excited to go back to work for 10 days. I was more excited to go to work, than I was to come home for the 4 days off.

After nearly 10 months since my loss, no feeling had come to me, nothing. I felt numb, no feeling, no miracle, no "ah this is why I had the felling to let them go". No answers to prayer, nothing was coming. Why was this happening? The feeling had guided me all my life for good, all good things in my life came to me when I had the feeling. Miracles came, wonderful things would happen. But this time, the feeling told me to let her go, and I listened like I did every other time. But it left me stranded, lonely and in a deep dark place. Darkness filled my soul, no light whatsoever, I would just listen to the natural man, by natural man I mean the natural instinct of the human body. I drank I smoked, and I indulged in all the basic instincts.

I was miserable. I prayed and prayed for the feeling to come and guide me. I prayed and asked why? I prayed for help, I had listened to the feeling like I always had before, but I had lost everything.

BY N.D.H

One night, I had a dream. I dreamt that I was walking along city streets, and I met a few people. I met families, and was very happy talking with them, I came across one woman with children and I stayed a while talking, and felt good in their company, but I moved on. They didn't want me to go, but I felt that I should. I carried on walking, looking around and then I saw her. I only saw the back of her, I did not see her face. I saw a petite woman with long black hair, wearing a white dress. Then a voice spoke to me and said, "This is your princess".

I woke up feeling great! I really believe that this was some sort of answer, some sort of communication from the Universal Energy.

I really believed that I would meet a girl. A petite girl, with long black hair, and this girl would be my princess.

The relationship between my wife and I was bad. I still couldn't see, or speak to the children. This upset me a lot. Time went on and still no sign of my princess. I came across a painting by Palla Jeroff, of the desert girl. It was exactly what I saw in my dream. The back of a petit girl with long dark hair, wearing a white dress. It was the exact same thing! It reminded me of my dream, and the voice saying this is your princess. One time I came home from my 10 days working roster and sat on the floor of my apartment. I wasn't drunk, I was just sad and lonely. I knelt there alone, in my empty apartment, and cried. My wife wouldn't let me see my children,

I was lonely and confused, the feeling had led me to this, the pure feeling of energy, that I knew came from the Universal Energy, had led me to this lonely depressive state ? I cried, and in my tears, I prayed.

I prayed and asked where is my princess lord ? Where is she then ?

To which a voice answered, quite clearly "she is on her way". I really did hear a voice. Not in my ears, not a vocal voice, but the same voice that I had always heard. I always heard it when the feeling came, a very still voice, even a silent voice if that makes sense? I was sure of it. I called my mother and told her, "Mam ! my princess is on her way !" I told my brothers, I said "lads my princess is on her way". They laughed and probably thought I was crazy. But I knew it, she was on her way.

Again time passed, and no sign of my princess. So I just carried on doing what I was doing. Until one night I was invited to a party in the city. My brother and his girlfriend came, and I was the third wheel, but I went anyway. My brother's girlfriend said to me   "go over there and tell those girls that were here, and I will be there in a moment", so I did. I wasn't afraid, and I wiggled through the crowd of dancers over to the group of girls my brother's girlfriend told me to go to. I finally made it through the crowd, and arrived at the group. There was a small petite brown girl there, with long black hair facing away from me. I tapped her on the shoulder, and said "hey", she turned around at which seemed like slow motion. Her long black hair waving behind with the twist of her head. She looked up at me with eyes that were filled with light, and said to me, "do I know you ?" I was still, and a voice in my head said "No, but you will".

I could write another book on the following events that occurred since that night.

If you believe in true love, magic, and the universal energies bringing 2 people together in the most unlikely circumstances, and against all odds. The next book will explain how the feeling came back. And how it kept telling me something, the opposite of which was actually happening in my life.

And most of all, how my life has grown and changed in an exponential way in the year following the meeting of my princess.

A true love story never ends.

I apologise for the grammatical errors in this book. It's not intended for eloquence, but rather to reach out to people who have gone through similar experiences. To let them know, that when life seems so bad and so unfair, that they should just keep going. Take the step one day at a time. There is always light at the end of the tunnel. The sun will always rise again. As Annie sings "The sun will come out tomorrow, bet your bottom dollar that tomorrow, the sun will shine"

To Be Continued .....

Printed in Great Britain
by Amazon